A.

ABOUT

FACE

Another visit to the planet Cobblers

by

Alec Hawkes

An ordinary bloke

Copyright © 2014 by Alec Hawkes

Published by Alec Hawkes ~ April 2014

ISBN-13: 978-1497574120

ISBN-10: 1497574129

~~~~~

Alec Hawkes asserts his right to be identified as author of this work in accordance with the Copyright, Designs and Patents Act 1988. All rights reserved.

Without limiting the rights under copyright reserved above, this book must not be sold or distributed by any person or persons other than the seller or sellers authorized by the above author and publisher.

~~~~~

Cover illustration by Derek Roberts

So many things that do not make sense - so much corruption ...

BANKS

GOVERNMENT

POLITICALLY CORRECT NONSENSE

CRIMINALS BEFORE VICTIMS

GREED AND POWERLUST

-

This, the third book in the series, joins ...

Common Sense Would Be Good

And

If Brains Were Dynamite

Foreword written by a check out girl

Acknowledgements

Many thanks go to the hundreds of members of parliament, and other governing bodies throughout the world, who continue to fuel the idea that they are less than honest, that they care more about their own political party and making money, than the interests of the country and it's people. Or indeed the interests of whatever particular country and people that they claim to represent.

No thanks at all to the completely divisive groups of politically correct idiots who continue to fuel the idea that those of us who debate things on a sensible level are in some way intolerant. These people are around in every country of the world and many hold positions of power. Sadly, they have indoctrinated many ordinary folk who will do anything to stifle any kind of debate as they promote their narrow agenda of total nonsense. These fools, well meaning though some of them might be, are as big an obstacle to creating a fair and tolerant society as self serving politicians and corporate corruption.

Nonsense and corruption appear to hold the upper hand at the present, it really would be quite marvellous if common sense and fairness could stage a fightback, and perhaps take over. We'll see...

Anyway, the main aim of this, as with my two previous books in this series, is to cause a few chuckles, as well as to provoke some thought. So, I would like to thank – in no particular order – the following ordinary folk who continue to provide me with useful material with which to (hopefully) create a witty little read for you, yes that's YOU.

Simon, Maddie, Marina, et al dans La Wheatie; Viv, a view from across the pond; Swaroop, a view from across another pond; Reg, Gasbag, Sir Colin J Rust, Linda, Pilgrim, Anne, Terry the Gooner, and a couple of farmers. You all know who you are.

Many thanks also to The Windsor Geek for technical know-how; Liz Mills, who formatted the manuscript for publishing; and Derek Roberts for the cover artwork.

Special thank-you's to Sharon, Eva, Georgie, & Chuck.

Foreword

What can I tell you about Alec? I didn't go to school with him. I have never worked with him. I know very little about his personal life and we do not have any mutual friends. We met briefly during his 'End to End' walk during 2013, and I'm not even interested in politics! I am not famous and I don't even have any of my writing published, yet. So why should I be the one writing about this author and encouraging you to read his work? I hope the next few lines will answer that question.

I 'met' Alec playing Scrabble online. I regularly beat him, sorry Alec. But he keeps coming back for more, I don't know why. During the last couple of years I have gotten to know Alec quite well, and the one word that comes to mind when I'm thinking about him is *passionate.* You need to be passionate to put on your walking boots, held together with duct tape for the last 200 miles, and walk from John O'Groats to Lands End in all weathers. You need to be passionate to keep going, knowing you are raising valuable funds for charities who are struggling to provide services for people that this and previous governments have no interest in. You also need to be passionate and have a certain strength of character to challenge the powers that be, despite being just an *ordinary bloke.* Most importantly, you need perseverance when you keep being beaten at Scrabble by a woman who works on a supermarket checkout!

Most of us, me included, watch the news and read the papers and moan and shake our heads at what we see and read. We know we are being lied to and treated like idiots, but we say nothing and just plod on with our daily lives. We are working harder for longer, for less and less reward and we are facing an extremely uncertain future. Maybe it's just me, but I fear my old age. Retirement seems like a distant nightmare at the moment, if I get there. Without people like Alec to pick up a big stick and poke those in control of our lives we have little or no voice. The ballot box seems to me as if it has lost it's power. Who can I vote for when they are ALL self-serving, pocket-lining liars?

All this could lead you to believe that Alec's work is as dry as dust. Far from it! What makes Alec's writing different is his inherent sense of humour. He tackles the biggest issues facing us in the UK ,and beyond, with glorious badinage (this is why I score so well at Scrabble). I challenge you not to chuckle while reading Alec's view of politicians and the havoc they wreak on us all. Alec is the first to admit that he may not always meet the standards he expects of himself when writing his books, but that matters little when his over-riding message both amuses and informs his readers. Enjoy the book!

Lynda Jones B.A. (hons)
English Language and Literature,
and checkout lady.

This book is dedicated to my English teacher, Mrs. Weller. She inspired and helped me more than she knew.

Also, to the late Mr. Moyle, Master of the Upper School. He gave me the freedom to express myself, he absolutely encouraged it. A very fine teacher, a decent man.

To both of you, thank you.

For those not entirely familiar with the English way of speaking English, and our many colloquialisms, I will offer translations periodically along the way.

Preface

This is my third book in the series, the first two being *Common Sense Would Be Good* and *If Brains Were Dynamite*. The first one, with all its errors, apparently flowed much better than the follow up. In this, I will attempt to produce a polished book, that also flows well. My aim is to cause eyebrows to raise, and for chuckles to be had.

Almost daily I, and I'm certain many other nobodies like me around the world, am fed a diet of total cobblers. Whether it be from governments, both locally and nationally, or from other folk. In this book, as with my first two, I aim to dissect much of the politically correct rubbish that we are force fed, and to do it in a way that, I hope, is humorous.

I am fairly sure that one of two things will happen on publication of this book;

Nobody, apart from a few friends, will take any notice. Or, the *PC brigade* will accuse me of being racist, sexist, ageist, homophobic, xenophobic, nasty, hate filled, stupid, intolerant, and blah blah blah drone drone blah.

It would be nice if both of the above were not quite true, and the book strikes a chord and raises a chuckle. We'll see. Remember, as you are now reading this, *don't take everything so seriously, particularly yourself*!

This time it's global!

Any similarity between any politicians living or brain dead, and the characters in this book, is entirely intentional.   Raaassspppp!!

Contents

Chapter One - Bombing, For Us? ... Page 3

Chapter Two - Cash From Chaos ... Page 27

Chapter Three - Arse About Face ... Page 47

Chapter Four - Shssh, They're Listening ... Page 69

Chapter Five. - Fat Chance ... Page 81

Chapter One - Bombing, For Us?

"Hey, is that Tehran? This is The US of A here, so listen up you shmucks and listen up good. We know you have some kind of notion that you can pick a fight with us and win the ball game, but let me tell you this buddy boy; we're the big guy round here, we're also the good guy, so don't be getting any ideas above your station, right!? Hey, is anyone there? You gone dumb pal? Cat got your tongue?"

"Hello America. No dumb here, we wait until you finish, loud mouth. You are bully boy, go away. We do not want fight, just leave us alone. Go drive away in your gas guzzle, or golf buggy. Don't interfere in Arab world, and don't call us 'Shmucks!'"

"Hey, we are trying to keep the peace pal, we don't wanna fight either!"

"Oh yes? Dismantle your weapons, take your soldiers away. Turn your gunships around and go home. Go play on your prairie. Goodbye."

"Now listen up buddy boy. Hey, are you there? They hung up! Mr. President, they hung up!"

Well, that was the US Secretary of State for Foreign Affairs Bob Bomber. Not quite the expert in diplomacy, but when were they ever? The president seems a nice, level headed kind of chap. What does he think?

"Bob, you can't speak to these people like that. We have to be diplomatic when we talk to anyone these days, especially out in the East."

"Yeah, I know that Mr. President, Sir. But these shmucks are making nuclear warheads, we know they have the capability. They have all that *deleted iranium* or whaddever it is. If we don't put on a show of strength and let 'em know who's callin' the shots who knows whad'll happen! Moscow? Bejing? Where's it gonna end Sir?"

"We will talk to the UN, leave it with me Bob."

******

These are indeed very dangerous times that we are living in. All around the planet there is posturing going on, the US threatening 'action' against anyone who flexes a bit of muscle, the Russians indulging in constant wars of words, while the Chinese continue to make money all over the place. The Untied Nations having a devil of a job to try and keep the peace. Mistake in the spelling there? Perhaps not, for what good purpose do they actually serve? If everyone in The United Nations kept to resolutions that are designed to encourage everybody to live and let live, in peace, then it would indeed be fit for purpose. However, we all know they don't.

Look at the 'big five'. Britain, America, France, China, and Russia. China and Russia hate America – oh yes they do! Mind you though, America hates Russia just as much in return so perhaps all is fair in the world of big boys being threatened by bigger boys. Britain, though still holding some kind of voice in the wider world, has extremely small armed forces these days after the German, sorry, EU led initiative, to render us impotent through constant meddling in our affairs, massive demands for money to finance the rest of Europe, leading us to 'skintville' and unable to fund a credible armed force. America has an insatiable thirst for oil and gas, and will stop at nothing to get it from wherever it lurks, and France. Well, France would far rather make wine than get involved in any world conflict, pretty much since the Maginot Line proved to be about as useful as a three foot high wall built of sand bags to stem the incoming tide off the wild coast of Cornwall. Yes, that's it – useless. We'd be total fools to rely on any United Nations resolutions to keep peace throughout our troubled world. This is why Untied, or Disunited, would seem rather more appropriate for a bunch of countries that have no desire whatsoever to get on peaceably with each other. What do they do anyway? Let's just take a peek shall we?

The latest meeting of The Disunited Nations Security Council, held in Switzerland. The big five are present, but also so are the rest. Everyone has been invited to this one, should be a great party. I wonder whose voices will be the loudest...

****

The opening speech from the secretary general.

"People of the world, we are here to talk of peace; peace for the world, for all the countries and peoples of the world. Whatever their faith, colour, race, or beliefs, peace for our world. No more wars, no more fighting, no more bigotry and persecution by the big man to the small man. No more bombs or guns or missiles, no chemical weapons. No occupations of neighbours territory. We can be friends, everybody can be friends with everybody else. If your neighbour is different then celebrate with him that difference, and he will celebrate yours. If your neighbour's religion is different to yours then pray with him and he will pray with you. If your neighbour lives a different way then live with him, and he will live with you. Share your neighbour's food and he will share yours. My friends, our world cannot take any more war and fighting. Live in peace."

Impressive speech Sir, lots of applause ringing around the hall. Oh, hang on, do I hear a whisper?

Apparently it was the Russians, they mumbled something in Russian. Sounded like they were a little 'cheesed off', so to speak. A translation is offered, by Igor Vodkaroff the Russian foreign minister.

"We are very happy to keep peace with everyone. Nobody interfere with Russian affairs and we don't interfere with anybody else affairs. Tell Yankee to stop spying on us. We do not spy on them."

Another whisper; well, more of a shout really. "Nuts!"

Time for the general secretary to step in.

"Please, address your comments and thoughts to everyone, in English."

"Yeah, okay buddy. I said 'nuts'. The Russians are spying on us, they always do. They spy on everyone. We have to do the same in return to keep an eye on what they are up to."

Ooh, another whisper, this one sounded a bit agitated. Maybe it was in Chinese? The general secretary is also getting agitated now...

"Please, everybody, you will all get your chance to speak. Address all comments to everybody. All microphones and headsets will be turned up so that everyone can hear everything, and all take part. The Chinese delegate, Mr Ker-ching, you are next to speak."

"Thank you. We in China are peaceful peoples, we do not want fight with anyone, not Russian nor American. Not

Arab, not European. We make peace, we make money. Everyone want make money."

"Nuts! You have armies as big as ours, not as good, but pretty damn big pal!" You know who said that...

"So, what about you, Yankee?"

"We have missiles and armies and airplanes, of course we do damn it, but that is to keep you guys in your place. To keep the peace." Interjection coming from Comrade Vodkaroff...

"So, you Americans are the ones to keep the peace, yes? You can have missiles, nuclear missiles, bombs, guns, all weapons. This is to keep peace? But everyone else must have no missiles, not even to protect them from you?"

"You got it buddy, glad you're seeing sense at last! We don't attack anyone, we are the greatest democracy on the planet, we keep the peace and spread the rule of democracy, the word of God."

" But you take oil and spread Yankee dollar!" Not sure where that little interruption came from, possibly one of the Arab delegates.

"Now just you hold on there buddy, we BUY your oil, we sell you munitions in return, so you can defend yourselves."

"Defend against who Yankee? You? Your puppets?" Time for the secretary again, before war breaks out – at the United Nations Peace Conference!

"Please, friends, everybody must calm down. We shall break for lunch."

******

Well, is that what happens at UN peace summits? It might just as well be for all the good that comes from their many talking shops. A whole load of waffle about initiatives for this, and initiatives for that, about keeping peace here and there and everywhere. While what actually happens is completely different. The ordinary people of the world, of just about every country of our world are absolutely fine with each other. It's the buggers in charge that are the problem. Look at the illegal and evil occupation of Tibet by China; we don't care. We just gave the Chinese the contract to build some new nuclear power stations in Britain. America doesn't care, they are busy colonising half the planet with the McDonalds Burger Army, including China. If they ask them to behave nicely then they won't buy the yankee burger. The European Union don't care, they'll be buying up the rights to Britain's nuclear power in due course. Oops, my mistake, we'll be *giving* it to them, of course. By that I mean Germany, obviously. And what of Russia? They don't care either, far too busy trying to lessen the power of the EU by forcing their former puppet states to rejoin them. As well as making mountains of money from their gigantic oil ocean and gas bubble.

By the time our new nuclear power stations are up and running in Britain it may well all be totally futile anyway, if a stray finger of madness or curiosity hits *the button,* the one that starts the ball rolling to oblivion. Maybe everyone at the top actually knows this anyway? We're all headed for destruction by a collection of greedy loonies, so just enjoy yourselves with whatever you can get your grubby paws on before the final balloon goes up.

I know we've been here so many times before, but was it total madness by God, Allah, The Boss, or mankind itself to create a fanatically religious people and stick them smack bang in the middle of a whole load of other fanatically religious people with beliefs that are so diametrically opposed to each other that it seems like a few mice have been housed in the middle of Cat City? The mice, admittedly, are big mice. They have sharp teeth and dirty great big feet, but the cats outnumber the mice by a massive margin.

History would have us believe that both the mice and the cats have equal right to this area, depending on whether we believe the version written by the mice, or that of the cats. The cats are hell bent (ooh, can I say hell? Don't want to offend those who don't acknowledge it) on the total destruction of Mouse Land, and the mice have an enormous army that will defend themselves to the bitter end by launching indiscriminate attacks on any cat cities, and countries, that threaten to threaten Mouse Land. Of course, the mice have friends. Their friends have even bigger armies with an enormous cupboard full of nasty weapons. They even have a macabre sense of humour; the friends of Mouseland sell the contents of the weapons cupboard to the cats!

Uncle Sam's Hardware Store; it sure does a roaring trade, yessirreee Bob!

The selling of weapons all over the world for people to defend themselves against other people who have no wish whatsoever to attack anyone at all, but who must do so because the 'elected' leaders in their particular country want to pick a fight with some other 'elected' leader who has been continuing the brainwashing programme designed to perpetuate the myth that other people from other lands are so different and so wrong that they must be taught a lesson? It does have something to do with that, of course it does, but mostly it's to do with resources that are in some lands but not others.

Vainglorious 'leaders' who have been democratically 'elected' by people who have been brainwashed into believing whatever cobblers (English word meaning nonsense, for the uninitiated) has been churned out in order to satisfy the lust for power and money. Many hundreds, even thousands, of years ago power mad loonies travelled the world in order to gain more power by seizing what wasn't theirs, and claiming it for their own. Before man invented engines and things that operate by the power of oil, it was largely just about the lust for power and territory. Now, sadly and glaringly obviously, it is mainly about oil. Oil equals money, money equals power, power equals corruption, absolute power equals absolute corruption. That old cliché, but as true now as it ever was. The so called Western democracies couldn't give a flying fig about unrest and wrong doings in the world, unless there is oil to be had. Remember all the trouble in Zimbabwe?

"Hello, is that Mugabe? Whitehall here old chap, London. Listen, we've been hearing that some pretty awful things have been going on over there, do you think you might see your way clear to stop it? There's a good fellow."

"Hello London. This is Mugabe office, Minister of Interior speaking. This is not Rhodesia any more, not Empire. We handle our own affairs, not you. Go away and play cricket, leave us alone. Affairs of Zimbabwe do not concern you."

"Well I do take your point old boy, but it's the Commonwealth you see. It doesn't look quite so good in despatches if one of our members isn't playing with a straight bat, if you get my drift?"

"Yes, I get your drift. Now drift off and leave us alone. Zimbabwe will look after Zimbabwe."

"Well okay old chap, just try not to kill too many of your opponents".

****

That told us, not that we care particularly; no oil to be had there. Sierra Leone, Rwanda, Syria, Tibet, some of the impoverished Baltic states of the former USSR, many places throughout our world where nasty things are going on, where ordinary people are suffering. Western governments don't give a 'monkeys'. No oil, no interest. They *do* give a bit of a damn about Syria, that is a strategic sea port; very useful for access to the oil rich countries nearby. There is, though, a well established tactic that is used by the West to pull the wool over a few pairs of eyes. Remember Iraq? Billy Liar and George Dubbya cooked up a goodun there! WMD, it actually stands for Wads of Mega Dosh, for a few, that is.

"I still say we were right to invade Iraq. We needed to get rid of the obstacle to making me filthy rich. I didn't lie to Parliament, I was merely economical with the truth. My wife, being a barrister, knows all about this tactic. It is perfectly legal, and anyway there were far bigger things at stake than just whether it was an illegal invasion. The future of my tenure as Prime Minister, my legacy, my personal fortune. These were the really important things. I am fully aware that people call me a war criminal, that there is blood on my hands. These people have nowhere near the accumulated wealth that I have, so *who cares* I say. Everyone knows that I'm a straight kinda guy. I mean, just call me Tony!"

Ha! Wouldn't it be nice if he *did* tell the truth? Fat chance, he'd have to have it beaten out of him. What does old Dubbya have to say about it now? George?

"Wibble."

Yes, well, I guess the lonely brain cell has worn out by now.

It would appear that the net of public opinion is closing in on old Billy Liar. But that's just public opinion. Nothing will happen to the cheesy-grinned fibber. The fortune we have to pay to keep him safe will still be paid, so many people who still hold positions of power supported him. Too much to lose. Maybe they'll give him a new identity so that any stray snipers can't try to take him out. How about Pinnochio? That would be a good idea, stick the Pinnochio puppet on a fairground stall and invite the public to throw darts at it, endless fun!

What did we get from the proudly self-proclaimed 'Heir to Blair'?

"The lessons must be learnt from the previous mistakes of previous governments. I am still reasonably popular with certain sections of society, and I need to protect that future legacy. Of course, if America insist that we must join in with their next bombing campaign in the interests of strategical point scoring over the Russians and Chinese, and the fine work of BP and Shell, then we'll put our best people on it to come up with a pack of lies and half truths to con the electorate as well as the wider world. Indeed, some of my best spin doctors have already written this speech for me to deliver to Parliament, though...

William, will you check to see if I have picked up the wrong speech?"

Whoops, Call Me Dave seems to be telling the truth as well. Pure fantasy, obviously. It does actually *appear* that current Western leaders are somewhat more ethical in their foreign policy, look at what the Americans said when they finally lobbed a few firecrackers at Syria.

"We are absolutely against the use of chemical weapons by anyone. We are going to bomb Syria and send the message that they cannot, under any circumstances, kill their own people with chemical weapons. If they want to use conventional weapons that are manufactured ethically in our very own Uncle Sam's Hardware Store to kill their own people then this is fine. This is ethical. We have never used chemical weapons, or weapons of mass destruction. Well, except for those two A-bombs all those years ago, oh and several 'experiments' that went horribly wrong in places like the Nevada desert. But apart from those, we bomb people ethically. It is for their own good to die in the cause of freedom."

Hmm, response from an ordinary Syrian civilian?

"Let's get this right then Yankee. You are bombing my country to send the message that my country should not bomb my country?"

"You got it pal."

"Oh, gee thanks for that."

"It's our pleasure. We continue to fight for 'Peace, Justice, and the American way'."

Then all the business in Ukraine, what was that all about?

"We in the Russian Federation must protect our interests. We have naval bases in Crimea. We cannot allow these to fall into the hands of The European Union. They are too close to Britain, and therefore America. Yankee pulls the strings in Britain, so they will soon pull the strings in Europe. We must act to protect Russian interests."

"Hey, you can't do that buddy, it's against international law!"

"Yes, that's quite right chaps. We stand with our American masters, I mean friends, that's against international law!"

"You are sore because we Russians wouldn't let you invade Syria, yes? Tit for tat? One law for you, bendy stretchy law? Another for us?"

"Huh?"

It all seems rather back to front to me, arse about face. So many conflicts breaking out all the time. So many people having to die for what appear to be stupid, nonsensical reasons. Are they just 'smokescreens'? A whole lot of tactical manoeuvering in preperation for something? Time will tell methinks.

Over in Mouseland the Cats and the Mice are forever blowing each other up and justifying their actions with total cobblers.

"It is our land that has been ours since ancient times. You lot have no business here."

"No, it is our land since ancient times. You lot have no business here."

"We will throw bombs at you if you don't go away."

"We will throw bombs at you too."

"We will throw bigger bombs."

"We will throw even bigger bombs."

"We will kill more of your people."

"And we will kill more of yours."

… and so on and so on and so on and so on and so on and so on and....

Anyone want to tell me that we are living in an enlightened age? An age where all cultures, all religions, all races live happily together and respect each other's differences? Ordinary people would, if they had the chance to. Trouble is, the people who would perpetuate hatred due to ancient differences are still so prevalent, and their doctrine is continually passed on to the next generation. Another place not so far from England still has a lot of nonsense spouted.

"You can't march down this road with that flag in your hands. This is our area and we march down it with our flag."

"Well it used to be our area before you nicked it, so we think we should march down it carrying our flag and you can stick your flag somewhere else!"

"Your flag is the wrong colour!"

"No, ours is the *right* colour, it's yours that is the wrong colour!"

"But this is our area, our road, we always march down this road."

"Well it's not, it's ours. We march down this road, it's

tradition, a proud tradition."

"Well it's our proud tradition, we want to march down it with our flag."

Several heads need banging together, metaphorically speaking of course, there have been decades of totally pointless and brainless violence.

Of course, much complaining in the modern age stems from centuries of colonisation of many places. Is The British Empire to blame? Many Kings of England throughout the ages sending rampaging armies into neighbouring lands to destroy the culture of the locals. Is this why *some* Welsh, *some* Irish and *some* Scots hate the English? Is this also why *some* people in many other parts of the world hate the British? For after the Scots, Welsh and Irish were forced to be subject to the English, off we went around the world collecting colonies.

"I say Carruthers, this looks like a nice little island with plenty of stuff we can plunder, get the crickct stumps out and we'll teach the natives to play. I'll be Captain!"

"Aye aye Sir."

****

It's all coming back to bite us in the bum now. The thing is, though, Britain was colonised for centuries. As I've said before, most places on the planet have been colonised by someone, and certainly most of Europe did the colonising, not just Britain. Is it about time everybody grew up a bit?

"Thank you very much indeed Sahib, for being in charge of our country for so long and showing us how to play cricket, now bugger off!"

The big problem now is not so much that vainglorious 'leaders' want land to show how powerful they are, it's oil. There is also the problem that our world has become totally obsessed with materialism and getting everywhere very quickly. Just take a look in the skies, aeroplanes everywhere! Oil is needed in enormous amounts to fuel these great monsters.

Just imagine if much of the world's oil happened to be in the middle of Australia, in that *stinkin' hot frickin' desert* smack bang in the middle of nowhere, near that big rock. Imagine that there was no oil in the Arab states, imagine that there was no oil at The Poles, none in America, and none off the coast of Scotland. Suppose it was all in the middle of that stinking hot desert. The West wouldn't be in the slightest bit interested in beating the crap out of certain Arab states, or desperately trying to be friends with others. They wouldn't be endangering the balance of the entire planet by drilling at the frozen extremities, there wouldn't be too many Arabs shouting *great satan* at America. Oh no, it would be someone else shouting it...

"Hey yankee, what are you doing here in my desert then bloke? I was just having a nice peaceful walkabout and scouting a bit of bush tucker, then all this bloody noise mate! What is all this machinery and equipment for?"

"Oil buddy, we have bought the rights to the oil in this little desert of yours."

"Who you buy it off Mister?"

"Your government pal."

"It's not theirs to sell mate, what about us?"

"You'll be okay buddy, we're gonna call this place Little

Texas, you can get a job in one of the burger joints we're gonna build here."

"Huh? Hey, look mate..."

"Or one of our Vegas style casinos. You got lucky pal, we're gonna Americanize this whole place! What do you call it anyways?"

"It's called Belongerus...."

Imagine if the locals in the *stinkin' hot frickin' desert* don't want to be colonised by the yankee burger army and Vegas style casinos and dirty great gas guzzlers. Imagine if they put up a fight, so they can protect their homes, protect their way of life...

"Mobilise the USAF, yesssirree Bob, we're goin' in!"

"Hang on yankee bloke, just suppose the Aussie government *did* give you this desert, what if you don't find any oil, what then mate? What about the mess? What about our country?"

"There will be oil buddy, and there's also gas here. We're gonna frack!"

"Me and my mates think you should leave us alone and fuck somewhere else!"

"I said frack, not fuck!"

"Same thing mate, you fracked up your own place now you wanna frack us!"

"Progress pal, progress."

"Nothing will halt the relentless march of progress, the steam roller that drills mega holes deep into the planet, the steam roller that flattens the rain forests and melts the polar ice caps. We need oil, we need gas, we need it now, and we don't care a toss about the planet and what's left for future generations. We need to fuel our selfish lifestyle, jump on our airplanes, climb in our gas guzzlers and ride the freeway. Yeeehawwww!"

"Well Bob, what about the planet. What about eco systems that are destroyed by pulling down what is natural, what is vital to the planet's very existence, to human kind's existence, to the survival of all life on the planet?"

"Huh?"

The relentless march of progress then is it? Let's see if we can extract every single drop of oil out of the planet, wherever it lurks. Let's build millions of aeroplanes and fill the skies with them. Let's cut down every single tree on the planet and lay concrete over everything. Let's destroy the habitat of creatures that are vital to our survival. Let's slam dirty great mechanical drills into the polar ice caps and then, just roll the dice and see what happens...

Oh look, double six. We're fucked.

****

Some scientists will say that global warming is accelerating the decline of our planet and others will say it isn't. Some scientists will say global warming doesn't exist, others will say we are already doomed. Some scientists will say that global warming is good, others will say it's neither good nor bad but either way it's nothing to do with us, just the natural changing cycles of the planet.

Okay then, Mr. Clever Scientific Wallah, what chance do

all us nobodies have if you lot can't even agree?

One thing we absolutely DO know, is that dirty great big corrupt corporate bastards have total control over what is happening to the resources on our planet, and to us. Listen to what goes on in the boardrooms of the mega rich and corrupt...

****

The latest, secret, meeting of some of the world's richest multi-nationals – as they like to label themselves. The meeting is chaired by Algernon Corrupticus The Fifth, American property and oil thief, I mean *magnate*. The latest in a long line of big fat bullies who have so much money that they roll their cigars in ten dollar bills, because they can. Also present are Lord Swagbag, boss of the European Bank of Centralised Corporate Power, and a large and regular donor to the British Conservative Party, and Major Colonel General Largegob Bignuts, overall commander of The US Armed Forces.

"Hang on," you say. "Why is he there?"

Old Bignuts is present because the US military are actually in desperate need of some more places to bomb and beat the crap out of. Algernon Corrupticus The Fifth knows only too well that to increase his wealth, and that of his cronies, to mega zillions instead of mere zillions, some more oil and gas will have to be stolen from foreign lands. To do this successfully a large army with an even larger cupboard full of nasty weapons will be needed. Bignuts is very open to financial 'persuasion' as to the specific targets...

Right, back to the meeting of the mega crooks. Also present are the respective heads of all of the richest oil companies, as well as Douglas Mcbillions of Wal-Wart and several CEO's of the most powerful televisual bullshit corporations. Several bankers are present, and also government representatives from around the globe, who can report the events back to their respective parliaments. Bignuts has had ten thousand troops deployed around the perimeter of the building, just to be safe, and the foolish bloody idiots (FBI) have 'planted' agents within the building to make sure nothing is leaked and that government agents only report back with the official version, not the real one.

Okay, off they go...

"Are all the doors locked? Has the room been checked for listening devices and cameras?"

"Yes Mr Corrupticus, Sir!"

"Okay, Swagbag, you tell us how things are in Europe then pal."

"Thank you. Well, we have managed to subdue all the individual states within The European Union, all those that matter anyway. We have corrupted all the television companies and media outlets, so that the idea of a federal superstate can be portrayed as a good thing. Brainwashing has been almost completely successful, just the British remain to be brought into line. We do have several puppets installed in Britain, the trouble is, though, the British people seem to be still able to think for themselves. They are proving quite difficult."

"What the hell?! You're a Brit aintcha? What's wrong with these folks? I thought we'd gotten them Americanized, you get those BBC guys on the case. Tell 'em to up the pace and get the message across. We need the Brits to be on our side, for some reason half the world seems to like the Brits so we need them to get us across the gain line. Who's that guy in their foreign office, Vague? Get him on it!"

" Hague, Sir. He's their foreign secretary."

"Yeah, that's the guy. Don't they call him Twelve Pints or something?"

"He used to brag about drinking lots of warm beer when he was younger, Sir."

"Jeez. Well he should be easy then, fuel him up Swagbag, and get him to fix it for the Brits to join the rest of Europe. We can deal with one big Eurostate. We don't need the Brits going around spouting ethical and moral crap. We need oil, lots of it! And get those damned Australians in line too. What about the UN, are they still the same?"

"Yes Sir, still spineless."

"Good. Okay, our good friend from Saudi Arabia, Prince Sharemadollar. What's going on over your way buddy? What about those Iranians?"

"There is no problem there, people getting internet access all the time. They see American version of freedom and want some. A few peoples protest but nothing is big problem. Many countries fight amongst themselves, now that dictators removed."

"Good, good. Well if anyone steps out of line too far than I'm sure Bignuts here can sort them out!"

"Yesssirreee!"

"Right, Chi-tem-Rotten, how's the situation in China and

out that way then buddy? We need you guys to keep making new drugs to fill the superstores with, so the peasants are kept in a reasonable state of health after all the crap that our stores sell them to eat!"

"All going nicely with us in China Sir. We are gradually getting more of a hold in Britain too, so we can help bring them into line also."

"Good work pal. How about North Korea, are they a threat?"

"We have missiles primed and ready, aimed right at them."

"Good work Chi-Tem. And hey, Mcbillions, get some of your stores opened up over in Britain. Those guys need a real dose of Americanizing. See if you can takeover their Tesco thing, and buy up their banks too!"

"Sir!"

"We'll get your named upgraded to McTrillions!"

****

So there they are, a little glimpse of the world's richest corporate fat cats, plotting our future. Of course, we are all led to believe that presidents and prime ministers are in charge of our destiny. Believe that and you really do need to slip off through the looking glass with Alice. The fat cats appoint the leaders for us, the fattest of the fat that is. We can hold as many *fair and free* elections as we like, the mega rich need to let us 'play', allow us to think we have some kind of say. Or is that too cynical? Do we have a say? Are leaders appointed by the rich and powerful? You can make your own mind up there, while you still can, before the thought police come along and extract your mind for research into making robot peasants that only serve the state. Robot peasants that have no ability to think for themselves because thinking has been banned, and the only point to their existence is to serve the stinkingly corrupt state machine.

Ah, North Korea. Well, maybe the peasants with no minds in North Korea are happy? Maybe total ignorance is total bliss? I doubt it, very much. So do you.

Over the next few years many more things will happen to our planet, many things that will change it and change the natural mechanisms that keep it in a state to support and sustain life. Some changes will be at the hand of Mother Nature, but many will be at the hands of diabollically rich, corporate, selfish morons. The constant drilling into the surface of the planet to extract every last bit of everything that might possibly be used to fuel our selfish and unsustainable lifestyle, and fill the trouser pockets of old Corrupticus and his cronies with zillion dollar bills, will – sooner rather than later – surely damage the planet beyond repair. If people protest then corporate greed will inevitably lead to conflict. Then what? You know it, old Largegob Bignuts will mobilise the troops , get the tanks out of the garage, and the speech writers will be called upon to spin a whole load of almost believable lies for the peasants to swallow. Here is UN Commissioner Codswallop, living up to his name...

"With agreement between The United Nations and the Western Allies we are reluctantly having to enforce UN Resolution 9823 which states: ***The continuing illegal occupation of the area known as UN Resource Collection Point 47, formerly known as Alice Springs, will be ended by diplomatic means if possible. If all***

diplomatic channels have been tried and failed then the final option of force will be reluctantly activated in accordance with UN law 93, sub section 876 paragraph 9.

Meanwhile, in the *stinkin' hot frickin' desert...*

"Hey Mick, what can you see up that tree mate?"

"Hard to tell at the moment mate, just a lot of dust!"

"That's bloody likely it's tanks then mate, on their way here. Bloody hell, a load of tanks to wipe the five of us out! Can you see anything yet Mick?"

"I can now mate, bloody hundreds of tanks, and look up mate. Planes, bloody bombers!"

"We better get out of here, and quick. Maybe we can make it down to the coast. Should be safer there."

Not quite reality at the moment, but give them time...

Moving on, a clever little ploy widely used by governments and corporate crooks, *divide and rule.* It's been adapted somewhat lately, they create an awful mess in order to make money out of that mess. Come on, let's have a look...

Chapter Two - Cash From Chaos

Remember how a few, actually it may have been quite a lot, of bankers made bucketfulls of filthy dosh out of the so called *global financial meltdown?* Yes that's right, when all the poor people were told that they had to tighten their belts because the world's banks had bunged everything on the outsider in the 3.15 at Kentucky, and it got stuck in the stalls and finished last. So zillions of Pounds, Dollars, Euros and Rupees were stolen from ordinary folk to bail out the banks? Well that's nice isn't it, filthy rotten swines. But hey, they don't care, it's business. The system can't be allowed to fail.

"We're alright Jack, pull the ladder up!"

The bankers have a flash name for this kind of corporate swindle, but I think cash from chaos about sums it up. Just listen to the total ratbags...

"Put everything on the Pound collapsing, now pull it off, put it on the Euro. Wait, the Dollar is on the rise, kill the Yen. The Pound is back, buy buy buy! Get all we have on the wheat crop failing. Move it to oil, yes oil. No wait, gas. Buy gas!"

The world of banking is an exceptionally complicated one, as are those that are involved in insurance and pensions. The poor people are sold the con, it's a bright and shiny, very believable con, but a con all the same.

"Sign here Sir, yes that's right, in the box at the bottom of the page. Keep your signature completely within the box. Thank you, right, we'll do the rest."

"What's it for?"

"It's your life Sir, you've just signed it away to us. Well, not your ability to breathe, walk, talk, etc. But everything you earn from whatever jobs you do within your lifetime. Everything you earn will be taken away by us to fund our dirty great big burgeoning corporate playground."

"Oh, thanks. Who are you?"

"We are what's known as *the system* Sir. Oh don't be worrying yourself too much about it all, you'll get regular statements to tell you how much of your money we have managed to turn into gold bars to fund our lifestyles and keep *the system* running, and you'll get a beautifully bright and coloured, totally worthless, plastic wallet every year in which to keep your statements."

"Oh, okay then. Thanks Mr. System. Can I leave your system at any time? It seems a bit lopsided to me."

"No, you are trapped. Once you are in the system that is it, you're in it. Like I said though, there's no real need for you to worry. It's a good system, it works very well for us. Your only alternative is a park bench, a bottle of cider and some old newspaper to keep you warm, but the system will pay for that for you. See how good the system is?"

Sound familiar? Very familiar to many I would think. Some get away, but the great majority will never escape. It all makes it so very easy for the operators of *the system* if – once people are in it – they can be kept in it, pounding the treadmill. Listen to these two, one of them has been trapped in the system for decades, the other recently signed on.

"Hello mate, how are you? Is that a 'hamster' wheel that you are on?"

"Hello there, yes it is."

"How does it work then mate?"

"It's quite simple. You just put one foot on the wheel to start with, and by walking forward the rest of the wheel turns, so that it actually goes behind you. You put the other foot on and just keep walking. The wheel keeps on turning, so there is always the same amount of wheel behind you as there is in front of you. Come on, you have a go!"

"Thanks mate. Oh yes, it's pretty good isn't it! Does the wheel actually take us anywhere? The scenery doesn't seem to change at all, as if we walk ten paces forward but we don't actually go anywhere?"

"That's right, yes. We never get anywhere, we just keep treading the wheel so that we can stay in the same place."

"I want to get off. I don't like this wheel now you've said that."

"Well you can get off if you really want to, but it won't do you any good. You'll just have to stay over there in the corner. Come on, it's not such a bad wheel. I've been on it for forty two years now!"

"What's it called?"

"They call it *the system.*"

"Bugger the system, I'm going somewhere else!"

"Good luck then youngun, see you in a little while. You'll be back, they always are."

The system. It *can* work, but not for most of us, that's for sure. It works best for those that operate it, or even – horror of horrors – those who *own* the system.

"You mean someone actually owns this frickin' hamster wheel? This wheel that I have to tread for years and years and years just to stand still and go nowhere?"

"Yep. It's owned by a mate of Corrupticus, well, a few of his mates actually."

"You mean there's more than one?"

"Oh yes, there's quite a few. A bit like a syndicate."

"No, I'm not having it. I'm definitely going somewhere else. There must be something better than that, surely. Bloody system, it sounds rubbish to me! And who's this *Corrupticus* bloke? What do you mean, *Syndicate*?"

"They are the people who run the system. They look after us, sort of. You can't beat the system though. Many have tried, nearly all have failed. Good luck anyway, I'll see you when you come back."

So off goes the youngster, determined to beat the system. While the older chap just carries on walking the hamster wheel, getting nowhere. He's used to it though, resigned to it. He tried to get away himself, many years ago when he was young, but soon came back when the system sent out a search party to get him. He'll be on it for a few more years yet, until they say he can get off. But then they'll just put him in another part of the system. He won't really care by then, way past caring.

The operators of the system are very clever, and they have specially adapted versions of the system installed in many areas of the world. Some have resisted, but not many. The vast majority have little or no choice but to join the system and take their chance that maybe, just maybe, they can find a way out some day. Let's have a little look in one of the *system training centres...*

"Good morning applicants, and welcome to our System Training Centre. You have all been identified as being able to join the system and work with us to maintain it, perpetuate it, and keep those who don't understand it in their place."

"What are they called Sir?"

"Good question. We call them many things; minnions, peasants, workers, plebs, ants, or just *general public.* But we need these people, we need them to help the system run, so we must make it appear that we are working for them, that the system is actually treating them well and furthering their best interests."

"How do we do that Sir?"

"Another good question. Well, we have many different branches in this training centre, all of which are totally 'geared up', so to speak, for the maintaining of the system to keep the general public believing what they are told. To keep them believing that they cannot beat the system and that it's not worth trying anyway, because there is no viable alternative."

"Do we have a word for that Sir?"

"Yes we do. It's called brainwashing, it works!"

"So what do we get out of it then Sir?"

"Well dear boy, *we* get filthy rich on it. In time, if you do and say all the right things, you too will get filthy rich."

"I think I'm going to like this system, Sir. But how do we get filthy rich, exactly?"

"All of you come with me. I'll show you all the different departments that we have. Every single one is working toward the same goal, and that goal is to make the minnions do all of the work and – most importantly – make them believe that they are being well rewarded. Come on, follow me, I'll show you."

Hmm, this all sounds quite good, or is it a bit sinister? I suppose we ought to tag along and see what this 'system trainer' has got to show them.

"Right, here we are. This building here is all to do with property, or real estate – as they call it in certain parts. We can go in, quietly, and have a listen."

A training session for budding estate agents is just underway. Sir Dominic Smarm from the estate agents *Smarm Bluff and Connem* is taking the class. He is also a civil servant, the estate agents is his 'nice little top up'. Let's have a listen...

"Right then, here is how we work. We are in close collusion with those other splendidly corrupt components of *the system*, what we call *solictitors* and *banks.* Elsewhere within the building you will see the offices of *Cheat and Baffle*, multi-national law firm specialising in property, as well as many others. You will also be shown how the banking world works within the system, and we have representatives from that most splendid of corrupt world banks, *The Holy Shit Bad Credit* or HSBC to the general public. It's all really rather simple, to us, but we have a very clever way of making it seem *very complicated indeed* to the public. You people in this room have all been chosen for your apparent aptitude for selling the product, as it were. Your ability to sound convincing. We have a technical term for this. Does anybody wish to hazard a guess?"

"Is it bullshit, Sir?

"Well done, yes, you will go a long way young man! So, bullshit is a vital part of the strategy for maintaining the system and making us all filthy rich. Of course, there is a system within the system, a sort of hierarchy. Anybody?"

"Rungs of a ladder Sir?"

"Well done, yes. You young fellows are on the bottom rung at the present, but with careful honing of your technique, and listening to how the masters of bullshit deliver that bullshit, you can steadily climb up the ladder. If you work hard, and develop your technique for delivering lies in a baffling, yet convincing way, who knows some of you may even make it to the heady positions at the top of the tree of corruption and terminal bullshit!"

"What are they Sir?"

"Oh, positions like bank manager, you could be pension fund managers, oil and gas company executives, Chief Executives of television companies, NHS managers..."

"What's NHS Sir?"

"It's the Nonsense Health Shambles. It only operates here in Britain, and let me tell you – *it's a very good earner indeed* for those who can master the technique of total bullshit!"

"Will we need to use it ourselves Sir?"

"Oh yes, you can use it very well to your own advantage!"

"I mean, will we need to use it for our healthcare if we get ill?"

"You have much to learn dear boy. It is only for the poor people. It is paid for by the poor people, used by the poor people, and we make money out of it."

"That sounds very clever. So where do we go?"

"Oh dear boy, we have private healthcare. It is far better."

"Who pays for that then Sir?"

"The poor do. Brilliant, isn't it!?"

"But if the poor are poor, Sir, then how do they pay for our private healthcare?"

"They pay for it in many ways dear boy. They pay through their bank charges, their housing costs, whether they be mortgage payments, rent payments, house insurance, buildings insurance, estate agents fees, solicitors fees, pension payments, life insurance, job protection insurance, mortgage insurance, fuel tax, road tax, alcohol tax, tobacco tax, value added tax. We are trying to add some more taxing ideas to the list."

"What like Sir?"

"We are working on a 'thought tax', that could be most lucrative. We are already a long way down the road of creating a *Thought Police* force. We just need to develop a way where people who think the wrong things can be taxed to the hilt for thinking it."

"What sort of wrong thoughts Sir?"

"Anyone who dares to think bad thoughts about the system!"

"And what about the banks and solicitors, and the other parts of the system then Sir?"

"Sir Jeremy Slimeball of the *Holy Shit Bad Credit* will explain about the brilliant roll that the banks play in the system. Jeremy, over to you Sir."

"Thank you. Well, I'm sure many, if not all, of you here will have bank accounts. A show of hands...Good. It looks like all of you budding young con artists have bank accounts. Well, we are one of the most important components in the system. We have ensured, over the last few years, that nobody can function in any way at all without a bank account, so in effect a bank account is now compulsory. We have everybody pretty much where we want them. Trapped in the banking system. We then systematically steal as much money as we can possibly get away with from everybody who banks with us. Not everybody will bank with the *Holy Shit bad Credit*, but we are in league with the other banks so it's all good, as they say in 'Peasant Street'."

"How do you steal their money Sir Jeremy?"

"Good question young fellow. We have all sorts of tricks up our sleeves, many of which are linked to the economy."

"The economy Sir?"

"Yes, they call it the economy. But it's real title is the property market. Without our lovely, glorious, bloated, corrupt and wonderful money making property market the economy is nothing. We trap people in the property market and it's a marvellous trap, they can't get out, ever. We love it, it's perfect. It makes us billions, even trillions!"

"But how, exactly, Sir?"

"Well we lend the general public's money back to them with hideous rates of lovely interest attached. It takes them forever, most of their lives in fact, to pay it back. We also have these wonderful things called *pensions.* These used to be a way for the peasants to keep a roof over heads in their senior years, but not any more!"

"Why is that Sir?"

"Because we stole all the money! We realised many years ago that these things actually *were* worth a good bit of lovely, filthy money. So we had to change things. We now have virtually all of the money in the peasants pension funds completely dependant on the performance of banks and everthing bank related. We cream off all the big lolly throughout the term of the pension, and leave the peasants just enough to stay alive. It's brilliant, it works perfectly!"

"Is that entirely fair Sir?"

"Fair? FAIR? Don't ever utter that word again boy, it is banned! There is no mention of 'fair' in the system, none at all. Fairness is banned. That is your first and last warning. If you mention it ever again, or even think it, you will be sent back to the peasants to walk the hamster wheel!"

"Sorry Sir."

"There are many, many more aspects to *the system* and we will cover these fully as your grooming progresses. There is the media, which is enormously powerful and influential, and our favourite little pets. The very best of you may even get the chance to become one of those lovely little pets."

"What are they Sir?"

"Politicians my boy, politicians."

****

The system. Lovely isn't it. Almost everybody gets trapped within the system, certainly us peasants do. Those that operate the system get very rich on the back of our efforts, which we have no choice but to continue with. The media churns out daily hogwash, cobblers, rubbish, nonsense – call it what you will – that the peasants largely believe. Some don't, but that doesn't matter because those that see through it are still trapped anyway.

The televisual nonsense boxes churn out shiny and colourful cobblers that keeps the peasants in their place and becomes quite addictive. It's designed to be just that. The agenda of the system is constantly launched at us with the force of a howitzer. Listen to this, a little bit of televisual hogwash...

"Good evening America, and good evening to the whole world. This is Channel 5000 New York broadcasting to the planet. I'm Dave Mouthpiece and we're coming right at you from Uptown Manhatten. Have we got a great show lined up for you tonight! By God we have. We've got Congressman HeadCrook dropping by to tell everyone how well the economy of the US, and therefore the whole world, is doing. And by God it's looking like everything is a bright red shade of rosy pink! We've got little Georgie Boy Osborne from the United Kingdom joining us for a chat about money and bullshit, and we also have some really great acts that will have you reaching for your credit cards and dialing us up. Yes folks, we're gonna get you all maxed out way beyond your limits. But don't you worry about that because it's gonna be fun fun fun all the damn way. Okay, all that's coming right at you after a few words from our sponsors. Don't you go away now, stay right there glued to your screens and we'll be right back with ya!"

****

Sounds pretty much like the televisual cobblers in Britain, just with brass knobs on. Actually, it sounds pretty much any old cobblers they churn out on televisual idiot boxes all over the planet. Oh well, it's all part of the system and it's all for our benefit. I suppose we ought to listen to the sponsors. Oh, that's adverts by the way...

"Hey, have you ever wondered just how you can get that nasty chemical stain outta your pants or skirt? That one that was caused by the piece of crap you bought to eat in the store? Well we have just the product for you! Not yet available in stores, we can now offer another piece of crap to get the other crap outta your pants, skirt, or any other garment that you purchased in Wal-Wart. You know those garments that were made in those little old slave houses in the third world for a nickel, and the slaves got paid half a nickel, and here in the free world our very own Wal-Wart sells for fifty dollars? Yes folks, they're the ones! Okay, here's what you do. You take this totally original patented product and lay the garment over it. You press the little button on the side and as if by magic out comes a jet of blueberry flavored toxic chemical liquid. This chemical crap will sure as hell remove the chemical crap from your garment as you gently rub the compound into your garment. This is 100% guarenteed to work, or we'll GIVE you another totally authentic garment identical to the one that you spilt chemical crap on. This product is a must have for every home and is only available by calling the premium rate number shown on your screens now. At a knockdown introductory price of one hundred ninety nine dollars and ninety nine cents you just cannot lose. So get yours today!"

I say, sounds like a bargain. I hope we'll be able to get them in Tesco! Should be okay I reckon, Tesco sells an awful lot of food with chemical rubbish in it...

Oh, the next advert is on. Oh look, it's a bank...

"Come and talk to us at the Sky High Bank! We can help you with absolutely every little need that you have. Whether you need a loan to pay back other loans that you took out to clear some previous loans, or whether you want to get yourself stitched up for life, this is the place for you. Oh yes, we got so much money that we just don't know what to do do with it all. We wanna lend it you, yes that is correct – YOU! It used to be your money, but we are the bank that likes to say 'Yes Sir, the Sky is the limit.' Come and talk to us about real estate, pensions, insurance, health care. You name it, we got it. We'll get you all maxed out as high as you like. Remember our buzzword folks, 'The Sky is the Limit.' Call the premium rate number on your screen now!"

I wish I'd gone to make a cup of tea now, don't much like these 'sponsors'. No matter, seems like Channel 5000 is back...

****

"Welcome back to the show. Well folks, you know how everything hit rock bottom a couple of years back? We got Congressman HeadCrook from the government with us right here in the studio to tell us all how things are on a big upward curve. Congressman, over to you Sir."

"Thanks Dave. Good evening America. Good evening world! Yes Dave, you are right there buddy, the US and world economy is now such a beautiful bright red shade of rosy pink that it looks like the cheeks on a cute little doll! We got so much money printed up that we just do not know how to use it all. But don't you worry your pretty little heads out there in 'voter land', we'll sure as hell be throwing enough of it your way!"

"Um, if you don't mind me saying so Congressman, did that sound like the promise of a bribe?"

"You got it buddy. That's damn right. I got my notes here and that's just what it says. I'll read it to you. It says 'offer bribes to keep the people sweet. Don't worry about our core voters, throw the bribes at those who don't traditionally vote for us. Win them over with sweeteners.' Oh, maybe I just read out the wrong bit..."

It seems like old HeadCrook definitely *did* read out the wrong bit! It obviously wouldn't happen, but wouldn't it be a great eye-opener if we could get the instant translation to the words of a politician. The politician reads out his or her carefully pre-prepared and very rehearsed bullshit about creating a society that is fair for everybody, and the translated version appears on the bottom of the screen.

Channel 5000 are now getting more 'words from their sponsors' at the moment, but when that's finished we'll go back and listen to Little Georgie Boy Osborne – with the *bullshit translator* installed to provide subtitles...

The television really is an enormously powerful weapon

for *the system* though. Whether it be Channel 5000 in America, or the BBC in Britain, or whatever channel in whatever country of the world, billions of us peasants sit down in front of it and get bombarded by all the stuff that the system wants us to hear and see. And, yes, much of it is believed by those who watch it. I'm not talking about the cobblers like soap operas that passes for entertainment, or the documentaries that show the better bits of mankind, or the movies that entertain. I'm talking about the news, the current affairs programmes. The ones where a certain agenda is pedalled in a certain way.

How many times do we see this kind of heart-rending stuff?

"Send two pounds a month to the number on your screen and you can save this little girl's life. She is only three years old and has to walk twenty miles to get a cupfull of water from a muddy puddle of poisonous, disease ridden water. Send your Pounds, Dollars, Euros, Rupees or whatever you have and you can save her life. Send some more and her mother can buy her some shoes from the nearest shop two hundred miles away so she can walk to the puddle in comfort."

Yes, it does tug at the heart-strings, it makes us peasants all feel so sorry, so guilty for the poor little children that can only drink from toxic muddy puddles, while we relax in our luxurious world of plenty. We send our two pounds every month. We feel better about ourselves. But why? Why are we doing this?

Please excuse my naivety, but hasn't America and Europe had the means to sort out the problems in impoverished places like remote African villages a thousand times? Oh, of course, I forgot. We in the *civilised world* only go to places to plunder the natural resources. We have just about all the ivory removed from elephants and the horns from rhinos, now nestling in our jewellery boxes or drug stores. We have many bits that used to belong to animals adorning rich ladies' necks and fingers. But while we were plundering all the goodies, why didn't we build a few reservoirs, build some irrigation systems, teach the locals about contraception? How many billions have we sent to Africa and other places over the last few decades? Are we really so stupid and careless and ignorant that we think that all the money and resources we send are getting to where we think they are going? Yep, it seems we are.

The *word* from the sponsor seems to have finished. Mouthpiece is back on. He's just introducing Georgie Boy. I don't think he's realised that the *bullshit translator* is switched on. This should be good, here's Georgie!

****

"Since our coalition government came to power in Britain in 2010 the prudent and tough decisions we have taken with our economy have enabled us to ensure growth within every sector. Business has been freed from the shackles imposed on it by the red tape of the previous adminisration, and is now able to grow and create jobs.Working closely with our coalition partners, we have ensured that the banks are working properly, and those that were bailed out with tax payers money are properly working towards a position where they can be returned to the private sector. Difficult decisions have had to be taken. But we have taken those difficult decisions and the benefits are now beginning to come through."

translation: *cutting the money we had to give to the poor has enabled us to give the banks a free rein. My shares are leaping up in value now, and I have secured another lucrative position on the board of a top bank. Soon we won't have to put up with those damn liberals either.*

"The completely independent Office of Budget Responsibility, which my colleague the Prime Minister set up shortly after taking office, has given us the thumbs up for our economic policies. I can now very confidently predict that our economy will continue to grow faster than any other within the European Union. My growth forecasts for the next few years will be 3.4, 3.8, 3.6 and again 3.6. We have turned around our ailing economy and we are reducing the deficit in a prudent manner. The housing sector in Britain is recovering well, and more and more people are getting onto the property ladder. Our policies are working!"

translation: *when we won the election my mate Dave created this muppet office to replace the previous muppet office. Most of them in there are our mates, even the labour 'plants'. Clever hey? They have said that I can say any old cobblers I like, they'll verify it. We have told the banks to give out some tax payers money for poor people to buy houses so we can give the impression that the economy is booming. It isn't. We have just kick-started debt growth.*

"Indeed, in the wider world we are looking to invest in much more sustainable energies. We have just managed to secure some much needed investment in Britain."

translation: *after giving all of your money to the banks we realised that the country as a whole is actually far more skint than we thought, so in desperation we went and crawled to the Chinese. They will shortly own what little we have left in the way of utilities.*

"We are continuing in talks with The European Union and, if we win the next election in 2015, we will re-negotiate new treaties with The European Union that will secure a much better deal for Britain. The Prime Minister has given a solemn promise that we will then hold an *'in-out'* referendum. The British people will decide their own future."

translation: *we have not a cat-in-hell's chance of Germany and France agreeing, or the liberals and labour, so I'm just saying any old cobblers that makes me sound plausible. We need some cracking good fibs to nullify the threat of UKIP.The British people actually have no say whatsoever.*

"Okay, thanks for that Georgie Boy. A very interesting little insight into the UK government. This is Dave Mouthpiece at New York's very own Channel 5000.We'll be right back after another word from our sponsors!"

Another one? Jeepers. It sounds just like our very own ITV; advert, advert, advert, advert, oh look – eight minutes of actual programme – advert, advert, advert.... click! That's that turned off, bloody rubbish.

There it is then, the system. Confuse the peasants, lure them in, keep them in, make them work their backsides off. Create chaos. None of us quite knows what exactly is going on, while a few make shed loads of money out of all the chaos. Nice.

Still, all is fair in politics and big business...

"Did you say *fair* boy?"

"Sorry Mr. System, Sir."

****

Right, let's look at some more enormous cons. The legal system, religion, more ways to confuse and brainwash us peasants. More ways to part us from the meagre amounts of money that we might be fortunate enough to accumulate. Many more ways that those in charge will con us. How much is actually arse about face? How much skulduggery goes on within the ranks of those in power?

Before we do though, this may well be of use to some. A glossary of terms.

Cobblers – *slang, nonsense.*
Loony – *crazy.*
Billy Liar – *former British Prime Minister, fibbing champion.*
George Dubbya – *loony.*
Waffle – *verbose, but aimless talk.*
Bullshit – *coarse slang, nonsense, pretended knowledge.*
Maginot Line – *wafer thin line of defence, unfinished. France 1939.*
Arse – *slang. Ass, butt, bottom.*
Codswallop – *slang, nonsense.*
Call Me Dave – *nickname, current British Prime Minister. Designed to 'de-posh'.*
Shmuck – *slang, derogatory term.*
Buggers – *unpleasant, awkward.*
Belongerus – *slang, Australian, native. It's ours mate.*
Pinnochio – *puppet, liar, long nose.*
Spin Doctor – *expert purveyor of bullshit.*
Nuts – *slang, US. I don't agree, go away.*
Wibble – *slang, making no sense at all.*
Fibber – *see bullshit, spin doctor.*

Chapter Three - Arse About Face

"The court will rise."

Ooh, looks like a case is just starting, this should be good. British justice, the finest and fairest in the world. I'll just give you the main protagonists, then let them get on with it.

This is a magistrate's court in *Middle England*, somewhere between London and Manchester. It could be anywhere really, there are a great many of them, but this one is in Central Cobblers, coming under the jurasdiction of Greater Nonsense County Council. The chief magistrate, or *chairman of the bench,* is Mr. Ralph Deadhead, brother of Dennis. His two 'partners' on the bench are Mrs. Molly Coddle and Ms. Caroline Tickbox. All three of these fine upstanding people worked their way through the ranks at Greater Nonsense County Council under the watchful eye of Ralph's brother Dennis Deadhead. He is the leader of Nonsense. All three have MBA's in political correctness.

On trial today is John Goodsense. Strangely, his daughter Chloe put him there. Anyway, let's listen. Here's Ralph, addressing the accused...

"Are you John Goodsense of 56 Hardknock Street, Central Cobblers?"

"I am. But I shouldn't even be here. This is just rubbish!"

"You will have your turn to speak. Firstly we will hear the charge, or charges. Our resident solicitor, and legal advisor, is Mrs. Stonewall."

"Mr. Goodsense, you are in court today to answer the charges brought by Ms. Chloe Goodsense against yourself. You are charged with the following: 1. *that you did willfully and intentionally force your daughter to walk to school. 2. that you did willfully and intentionally force your daughter to eat a proper breakfast before she left for school. 3. that you did willfully and intentionally prevent your daughter from watching satelite television and using the internet after eleven p.m. And forced her to do her homework instead. 4. that you did willfully and intentionally withhold her daily allowance, or'pocket money', therefore preventing her purchasing sweets, fizzy drinks, and burgers. 5. that you did willfully and intentionally withdraw the daily allowance mentioned in charge four which led directly to her being forced to offer 'favours' during school hours in order to provide her with the finance you had withdrawn. 6. you have willyfully, intentionally, and blatantly infringed yout daughter's basic human rights in all of these areas.* How do you plead?"

"Not guilty, it's all rubbish! Total nonsense, she's only thirteen. Surely I know what's best for my own daughter!?"

"Do you deny the charges, Mr. Goodsense? Do you deny withholding her pocket money? Do you deny making her walk to school? Do you deny making her eat a proper breakfast? Do you deny withdrawing her access to satelite television?

"No, I don't deny any of that."

"So your plea is guilty. Thank you Mr. Goodsense. Mr. Chairman, other members of the bench, the plea is guilty."

"Thank you Mrs. Stonewall. Mr. Goodsense, do you have

legal representation?"

(a smartly dressed young woman stood at the side of the court gets up, holding a clip-board laden with pieces of paper).

"Your Worships, I am the duty solicitor representing Mr. Goodsense and he has advised me that he pleads guilty and has nothing further to say, except that – and I quote – he was *'acting only in his daughter's best interests'*."

"That's bollocks, I didn't say that at all! And that woman is not representing me, if there's anything to say for me then I'll bloody well say it!"

"Mr. Goodsense you will moderate your tone, and your language, or risk being ejected from this court and held in contempt! Duty Solicitor, are you representing Mr. Goodsense, or not?"

"Your Worships, there appears to be some confusion. I did introduce myself to Mr. Goodsense and advised him that his best policy was to plead guilty, show genuine remorse for his crimes, and maybe his punishment would be a little more lenient as a result. I thought he had agreed, so I proceeded accordingly."

"Thank you. Mr. Goodsense? Have you anything to say?"

"Yes, she did introduce herself and she did say she was the duty solicitor who was here to represent me. But I told her she was not acting in my, or my daughter's, best interests!"

"I see. And are you happy to speak for yourself without any legal representation?"

"Too bloody right I am mate! And it's not guilty!"

"Mr. Goodsense! A final warning to moderate your language!"

"Sorry."

"Okay. You may now answer the charges. Tell us why you committed all of these crimes against your daughter."

"Well I don't consider that making Chloe walk a mile to school is a crime. There are a few other kids from our street that walk to school. They could have walked together. I thought I was doing her a favour, she gets very little exercise as it is, except when she leaves her bedroom to raid the fridge!"

"And making her eat a *proper breakfast* Mr. Goodsense? What was the idea behind that little ancient old wives tale?"

"Well, my mother always gave me porridge, or boiled eggs before I walked to school. I thought it would be much better than her filling up on crisps and chocolate from the school vending machines. I thought she'd be able to concentrate better on her lessons with some hot , nutritious food inside her."

"And this misplaced *good intention* Mr. Goodsense, was this what led you to withdrawing your daughter's lawful right to her daily allowance? Her pocket money Mr. Goodsense. Is this why you stole her pocket money?"

"I didn't steal her bloody pocket money, I just didn't give her any. I pay her school dinner money through my bank, so she has no need for money when she's at school.

She has her mobile phone and I always make sure it's charged and has enough credit on it to phone me if she needs to. And I give her a card to use in a public phone box just in case she loses her phone. I don't see that she needs any cash at school. If she doesn't have cash in her pocket then she can't waste it on junk!"

"It seems that you don't quite understand, Mr. Goodsense. We have laws, people have rights, yes Mr. Goodsense even your daughter has rights. The law is enshrined in the human rights act Mr. Goodsense. You have clearly shown scant regard for your daughter's human rights. Your daughter has every right to be treated in exactly the same way as all the other children at her school. It is your duty Mr. Goodsense, as her father, to ensure that she has full access to all the things that all the other children have access to."

"I understand this your worships, but most of the kids at Chloe's school are unfit, overweight, over tired, and over exposed to television and the internet. I just wanted to give her a better chance. To give her a better, healthier life. I thought I was doing the right things!"

"Yes Mr. Goodsense, clearly that is exactly what you thought. But you are very wrong, and this court is here to decide if you have broken the law and infringed upon the human rights of your daughter. Clearly, Mr. Goodsense, that is exactly what you have done. This court finds you in clear breach of your daughter's human rights, and we think you will both benefit from a break."

"A break? What do you mean, a *break*?"

"Your daughter will be placed in care for a period. She will have provided for her all the things that you have been denying her. She will be allowed unhindered access to the internet and television, with all the educational benefits that they bring. There will be transport provided to take her to and from school, and she will have her daily allowance of ten pounds reinstated. You will be ordered to pay the sum of seventy pounds per week into a special account that will be opened in her name, added to which you will pay a further eighty pounds per week to pay for the transport that you refused to provide for her. It is grossly unfair to expect any child to walk to school in the twenty first century Mr. Goodsense. The streets are awash with dangers and your wilful neglect placed your daughter's wellbeing a long way down on your list of priorities."

"But this is just rubbish! What about..."

"As for you, Mr. Goodsense, you will attend a compulsory parenting course for six months in addition to being ordered to pay a fine."

(after consulting with legal advisor Mrs. Stonewall)

"You are fined the sum of five hundred pounds Mr. Goodsense, plus one hundred pounds court costs. In addition, you will pay the backdated daily allowance to your daughter for the six months that you have been withholding it. In total you will pay two thousand four hundred and twenty pounds, plus the weekly amount already mentioned to ensure that your daughter has what she is entitled to. You will pay at the clerk's office before you are allowed to leave today. Mr. Goodsense, you have narrowly avoided a custodial sentence with your neglect and abuse of your daughter. You have been let off very lightly, but you MUST change your ways. You have the six months of your compulsory council run parenting course, which we are providing free of charge I might add Mr. Goodsense, to prove that you can change your ways and learn to be a good and caring parent to your daughter.

You will be allowed to see her, at her discretion and convenience, during the period of your rehabilitation. Have you anything to say Mr. Goodsense?"

"This is rubbish, this isn't fair at all!"

"You will be held in contempt Mr. Goodsense. Officer, please escort Mr. Goodsense to the clerk's office and see that he complies."

Blimey, have things all gone a bit too far? I'm rather pleased I was a kid when we *didn't* have a whole load of so called *rights*. The days when mum and dad made the rules because mum and dad knew best. The days when I loved a good breakfast before school, very glad of it! The days when most of us walked to school, the days when playing and mucking about outside was infinitely more educational and fun, and character building, than being stuck in front of a television. They days when we ate proper food at school *and* at home, and the occasional bit of *fast food* was a very rare treat. The days when there wasn't a security fence around the perimeter of the school. The days when we didn't have closed circuit television recording every little movement inside and outside of school grounds. The days when the kids went to their lessons and kept their mouths shut so they could hear what the teacher was saying in order to learn things, or we'd get a clip round the ear. The days when we respected our elders purely because they were elders and therefore they knew more. The days when we learnt how to think for ourselves, after being shown and taught a few basic guidelines.

I know it wasn't all good back then, and it isn't all bad now, but it does seem that the question of *rights* and demanding them has tipped rather too far in the wrong direction.

****

It's not just magistrates and the civil courts that seem to have things around the wrong way though, and that's just in Britain. And don't even think about how corrupt the criminal courts are! 'Justice' can be paid for, bought by the highest bidders. We'll come back to that, but I suspect other parts of the world may have things similarly lopsided. Though, in some other parts of the world it will be completely the opposite again...

"Rights? What do you mean, rights? This is a dictatorship, you have no rights. Now go away before the state has you mysteriously disappear." And *that* could be in any number of 'tin pot' states around the planet. They don't need to be 'tin pot' states though, not if we – *The West* – were really interested in a fair world, as well as a fair place where we ourselves live, where we were lucky enough to be born. If *The West* really had wanted to help poor countries to embrace the idea of a fair society then they would have done so long ago. Maybe they want to help keep a certain amount of the world's population in the dark about what kind of life they could have? Maybe there isn't enough oil to share with everybody, so those with donkeys and handcarts with broken wheels will have to carry on as they are? Or maybe the folks in those kind of places are quite happy as they are and know all about the decadent ways of *The West* and think it is us that have a poor lifestyle? Intriguing question, that one. What would be sensible, surely, would be a decent balance everywhere.

Getting back to us, though, what about this for a dreadful thing that has gone on for decades, probably longer?

Another rather corrupt institution...

"Forgive me father, for I have sinned?"

"What have you done child?"

"I ran across the road without using the organised crossing where the lollipop lady stands, and when she called out to tell me off I stuck my tongue out and just carried on running!"

"Wicked child. You must say five *Hail Mary's* and pray for God's forgiveness."

Hang on a minute, let's swap them round shall we?

"Forgive me child, for I have sinned."

"Oh, really? What have you done Mr. Priest Sir?"

"You really don't want to know sunshine, but let's just say that me and some of my mates have been at it for donkey's years. And we best not even mention how some of the 'sisters' beat the living daylights out of so many kids, for nothing!"

Hmm, all in the name of religion? Which one might that be then? The *you are a child therefore you are wicked* religion? Maybe it wasn't all in the name of religion, but it was certainly used as a mask. For centuries mankind has beaten the crap out of itself in the name of one religion or another, remember this lot? Well, none of us would actually *remember* them, but we have all heard about it.

"Forward, men, in the name of God and our Lord Jesus Christ we will batter you into submission with all of our might!"

"Oh yes? Take that you bloody Christians!"

Yep, the *Holy Wars.* Nothing in the least bit holy about the so-called crusades. Maybe our forefathers didn't know any better way back then. Maybe they did, maybe it was just a case of trying to impose our customs and beliefs on those who were different? We'll never know now, not really.

Then we had the "I need to create a new religion just so I can get rid of my wife" cobblers made up by that big fat slob Henry VIII. So the Church of England was 'created' with new rules that enabled Fatty Boy to get rid of his missus and bring a new one in, hopefully to give him a son and heir to succeed him. His Holyness 'the bloke in charge in Rome' was not amused by that little ruse!

Then what? When Fat Boy slithered off this mortal coil and his daughters succeeded him instead of the longed for son, Mary towed the line with Rome, but she lost her marbles quite young and shuffled off to join daddy. So up stepped Elizabeth, and crikey was she in trouble! *'HERETIC'* they called her! She happened to be a reasonable person who didn't quite see why we all had to argue about which particular Sunday School club we were in, so to speak. It did seem to calm down after a while, as she parked her Royal bottom on the throne of England for more than forty years. But I'm sure you get the point.

"Non believer! Burn her, she is a witch, a bad witch! Duck her, if she floats she is a witch and must die. If she drowns then, oh, she's dead anyway."

We are, quite obviously, far more enlightened and tolerant now though aren't we. Aren't we?

"You can have that bomb in your face in the name of my God!"

"Oh yeh? Well you can have another one back in the name of my God!"

"And you can have a knife in your throat in the name of something else!"

"And you can have a knife in your throat for some other reason that is so old and worn out now that nobody can actually remember what it was or how it came about but you can have the knife in your throat anyway because you are not like us!"

How many wars were started over conflicting religions and beliefs? Clearly, a lot. Even today, supporters of certain football teams batter the supporters of rival football teams due to a deep-rooted hatred stemming entirely from differing religious beliefs. Ah, now there's an idea! Why not stop all the fighting over religion and have them all play a game instead? Not football, or soccer, or rugby – far too physical. How about netball? Yes, netball is relatively gentle by comparison, a non-contact sport. We could have the World Netball Religion Cup...

"Here is the draw for the first round of The World Netball Religion Cup. This is a totally global competition, and it is to replace religious dogma and ignorance. The ties will be played over two legs, with the teams at home in the first legs being called first. We have a canvas bag full of brightly coloured numbered balls, with the home team numbers being drawn by The Dalai Llama, and the away teams by a nurse. Here we go..."

"Number seven."   *(Seventh Day Adventists)*

"Will play..."

"Number four."   (*Hindus*)

"Ooh, tricky tie there for the Adventists, they'll need a good advantage from the first leg."

"Number ten."   (*Jews*)

"Will play..."

"Number two."   (*Buddhists*)

"The Llama is smiling there, should be a cracking good game that one."

"Number twelve."   (*Christians*)

"Will play..."

"Number one."   (*Jehova's Witnesses*)

"Could go either way that one."

"Number fifteen."   (*Mormons*)

"Will play..."

"Number six."   (*Rastafarians*)

"Battle of the underdogs there."

"Number five."   (*Moslems*)

"Will play..."

"Number sixteen."   (*Catholics*)

"Ooh, that one could be the tie of the round. Heavyweight clash there, it'll probably be the one that's shown live."

"Number nine."   (*Siekhs*)

"Will play..."

"Number eight."   (*TheMoonies*)

"Possible upset on the cards there."

"Number fourteen." (*Humanists*)

"Will play..."

"Number eleven." (*Spiritualists*)

"Could be some 'mind games' involved in the run up to that one."

"Number thirteen." (*Protestants*)

"Will play..."

"Number three." (*Druids*)

"Another cracking good game in prospect there!"

"Well, that concludes the draw for the first round of The World Netball Religion Cup. The first legs will be played during the first week that we can find which doesn't clash with any religious festivals. Midsummer will be ruled out, also, so those who wish to howl at the moon can do so. I'm very much looking forward to this, should be so much better than blowing people up because they have different religious beliefs. There are, it must be noted, two notable absentees from the draw. They don't quite have religious beliefs, but they wanted to pursue another avenue anyway. Let's see what's happening with them. It seems that General Myth is addressing the troops, come on let's have a listen..."

"We have spent many hundreds of years without fighting for our non beliefs, we have missed out on so much. So many people have had so much fun fighting for their beliefs, and so many have died as martyrs. Atheists, join with me as we march off to war to defend our lack of belief. The enemy is waiting for us, playing dirty tricks and mind games. Atheists, join with me as we engage in battle, and fight to the bitter end. The end that will provide ultimate victory for us!"

Crikey, sounds like they mean business. What's happening over on the enemy lines I wonder. Ooh, look, it's Colonel Notsure, addressing his troops. Seems he is sat on a fence of some sort. Good vantage point I guess...

"Stand fast men, wait until you see the whites of their eyes. Let them come to us, we will crush the Atheists for their non beliefs. Fight like your lives depend upon it. Agnostics, do not yield to the enemy. Do not falter in your steadfastness, remain on the fence until the very last second!"

Hmm, not quite sure who's going to win that particular battle. Maybe we'll pop back in a while and see how it's going.

****

There are, though, so many things that don't work the way they should do, the way the people in charge would have us peasants believe they work. It's not just a whole raft of different religions giving us completely different versions of how to live in a decent manner. The afore mentioned televisual boxes blast out the agenda. Everybody is just exactly where they want us. There is still, though, just about enough freedom left for a little bit of *say and think what you like*, but time may well be running out.

The press here in Britain mostly trot out the line of whichever particular political control freaks they support. But some mavericks are actually still allowed to voice their own opinions, must have slipped through the net I guess. That net is still awaiting someone to sew up the holes due to all the cutbacks...

Anyone at all in Britain is not allowed to say, or think, certain things. Listen to this...

"Immigration is brilliant, we need loads more of it. The diversity and richness of culture that we achieve by immigration to our country is of great benefit to us all."

Absolutely it is, virtually everybody except a few loonies would agree with that, the statement that is trotted out by the media and the government. Immigration is brilliant for every country. America, Australia, and Britain – to name but three – were forged almost completely by immigrants. I personally, and millions more like me, couldn't give a flying fig where anybody comes from, what shape, size, or colour they are. Nobody has any more, or any less, right to be anywhere. But listen all you politically correct fools (if any of you are still reading this), Britain is massively over-full now. Don't believe me? Look at what happens when Mother Nature sends the big storms and we are flooded. Yes, that's right, all the places that we have built on over the years that we shouldn't have been built on are submerged. All the flood plains that have villages, towns and cities built on them shouldn't have anything built on them, not if the people who are there are to keep their feet dry and their houses and gardens prevented from turning into giant muddy aquariums.

One only has to venture out onto any of our motorways. Absolutely overflowing with traffic, in many instances completely stuck, stationary, overheating. At the best of times the whole stupid network is balancing on a very precarious knife edge, just hoping that one little domino won't fall over and bring the other five hundred million dominoes tumbling down with it. Inevitably, several dominoes *do* tip over and, bang - twenty mile tailbacks all over the country. Why do we need to keep building more and more roads? To keep building more and more settlements where our ancestors worked out many moons ago that it wasn't safe to build? To keep squeezing more and more houses and flats in already over-crowded areas? One reason certainly has to be that our wonderfully moronic governments – all of them – over the years have been trying to increase their client base, their voters. But it's more than that, much more.

Here's London Mayor, Boris Johnson, telling us all how we must increase the traffic, ALL traffic.

"I firmly believe that, although we in Britain live on a tiny little island that is beginning to sink under the weight of people and concrete, and we have the busiest airport in the world bar absolutely none, we must increase capacity. We have super duper high powered jets taking off and landing at the rate of three every five minutes, and trains zipping around all over the place like a thousand little toys, but we must fill in the gaps. We have tunnels all over the place, indeed London is one dirty great big tunnel. But hey, let's build some more tunnels! We want to put tunnels under the tunnels and bridges over the bridges, motorways on top of the motorways and rails next to the rails. We have a few spare seconds of air space over our airports so come on peasants, let's fill in those naughty little gaps. Let's build another airport, let's build more runways at Heathrow and Gatwick, let's get *more* traffic in the air, and on the roads and on the rails. Let's increase the value of the shares that me and my mates have in all these hair-brained schemes that..."

"BORIS!! SHUT UP!!"

"What? Oh, yes, sorry. That was the PM, he was telling me to leave that last bit off. You lot aren't supposed to know that we in power make bucket loads of dosh out of having shares in all these things. So just ignore the last bit, pretend I didn't say it.

Right, I'll take a few questions. You, yes, erm, what's your face?"

"Joe Public"

"Okay Joe, what's your question?"

"Thank you Mr. Mayor. Please tell us how we can afford to build loads more roads, loads more over and underground railways, increase the amount of air traffic, increase the amount of road and rail traffic, therefore increase the amount of people coming in to the country, when we can't even repair the crumbling roads and railways that we have already?"

"Erm..."

"And we haven't got enough money or resources to care for our sick and elderly, but we can splash out billions on schemes to make our crumbling infrastructure even weaker?"

"Erm..."

"And the oil is running out. We burn what we already have so much faster than new stocks can be found."

"La la la la, roobarb roobarb, not listening, can't hear, la la la la roobarb roobarb."

Yes, thanks Boris. They really do think we are stupid. They must do. The government led by one of the biggest liars in history was on the brink of collapse in 2007, so

Billy Liar slipped away quickly and gave the keys to that biggest of all numpties Gordon Brown. He of the 'three plus four equals twenty nine million' sort of economic lunacy. That little charade collapsed very quickly, as it was guaranteed to do, and in came a new bunch of con artists to, *apparently,* clean up the mess. Well, some job they've done. The country and it's people our now more divided than ever. Call Me Dave and Georgie Porgie Finger-in-the-pie have spent four years shuffling debts and shafting various sections of society, while pandering to other sections of society, playing with our money. While all the time pleading that we are skint. But still, when a new scheme comes along to destroy another few miles of this formerly green and pleasant land with tons of concrete and steel, they seem to find another little stash of notes.

"Hey, look Dave. I've just found another piggy bank. It's full of filthy dosh!"

"Well keep it quiet George, we don't want the peasants knowing about it do we! Quick, trouser it!"

Totally and absolutely full, worse than that, over full. Britain will still be forced to take more people in, so will many other countries. But who can blame anyone for wanting to come to Britain? That's right, nobody. Maybe there is a solution, maybe if we stop destroying half the planet and all it's natural eco systems there will be room for everybody?

"Hey, mister, I wouldn't bother trying to come down here and live in our *stinkin hot frickin desert* mate. Not unless you like being too hot to even think straight. Then there's all the bush creatures that'll bite you and fill you full of all sorts of poison."

No, I don't think we'll go there, thanks. But there would absolutely be room for everybody if certain countries didn't steal all the resources from everywhere to fuel and feed greedy lifestyles. What do you reckon Boris? Mr. Mayor?

"Well I have the perfect solution. We are going to turn Britain into a water park. Southend-On-Sea will be renamed Southend-In-The-Sea, Henley-On-Thames will become Henley-Under-The-Thames and Wooton-Under-Edge will be Wooton-Over-The-Edge. We also have plans to rename The Somerset Levels as Somerset-Way-Beneath-The-Level. Not sure about Stoke-In-Trent, but that's in the North and we don't care about that. They're all bloody Northerners up there! Working closely with our partners in The European Union and The G8 we are going to create millions of new aqua towns, everyone can come to Britain and when they do they can all vote for me!"

Yes, well done Boris, burble burble...and they reckon he'll be Prime Minister one day!

Seriously though, Britain is massively over populated. Everyone wants to come here and enjoy the benefits of living in a welfare state with our Nonsense Health Shambles and other tax payer funded benefits. I don't blame them, who would? Anyone who dares to voice any doubts, though, about the continual multiplying of the population is called racist, or xenophobic. No, you numpties! The country is overflowing!

Still, nothing will be done because our masters in Europe have long since secured the deal where we have no choice but to comply, no say whatsoever. Nice one, well done Messrs Heath, Wilson, Callaghan, Thatcher, Major, Blair, Brown, and Call Me Dave. Every last one of the idiots signed away more and more power to run our own affairs, to have some kind of say in whether Britain can be a serious rival to Bangladesh and China in the *"let's see how many people we can cram in a phonebox that isn't anywhere near big enough"* kind of game.

"Ve are vell avare zat you von zee var you English fools, so now you pay. Ve fill you up till you are so squashed you can't move. All part of our masterplan."

You think I'm joking? I'm not, but I've probably 'nailed' it to be called a racist xenophobe now. Not true, nothing could be further from the truth. Britain is full. Many other places are pretty near full too. The countries that aren't full are the ones that don't have any money or resources to support any kind of population. Why? Might it be that any resources that might have been laying around have been plundered by The West? The so called civilised world squandered, and still continues, to squander them? Still, there's not much left in Britain to worry about now, truth be told. Our gas comes mostly from Russia, our oil comes mostly from Arab states, almost everything in Britain is now owned overseas, even our train companies.

"The next train on platform ten is overcrowded and badly ventilated with all ticket monies going to a company in France."

Oh that's nice. Even our football teams are owned overseas...

"Welcome to Franchise Rovers, today we have a potentially great game in prospect against Franchise United. This is a cup game in the sponsored *Bank of Many Rip Offs* cup, with the winners going on to play the victors in the game between Franchise City and Franchise

Town. The finals will be held at the Franchise Stadium at a time deemed perfect by the people who own the game, the satelitte television companies."

Oh, hang on, there's a knock at the door. Bugger, it's the *thought police.* I'm out of here. There are several off them outside my door, holding lots of clip boards. I better be quiet, they are listening...

Chapter Four - Shssh, They're Listening

"Hello, can I speak to Mrs. Nobody please?"

"Who's calling?"

"Is that Mrs. Nobody?"

"Yes, but who is calling? How did you get my number?"

"Your number is on the data base. We have all your details on the data base, we know everything about you. How are your husband and your three adorable children?"

"Look, who is this? What do you want? And how the hell do *you* know whether I have any children, or whether I'm even married? I demand you tell me how you got my number. This is my personal mobile phone, I don't give my number out to anybody except my close friends!"

"We know everything about you Mrs. Nobody. We know everything about everybody, all of the *nobodies.*"

"Goodbye, and DON'T ring this number again! Whatever it is that you are selling I don't want it!"

Sound familiar? I'm sure it does. That phone call could be taken pretty much anywhere in the world. ***BIG BROTHER IS WATCHING, LISTENING, RECORDING OUR EVERY MOVE. BE CAREFUL WHAT YOU SAY AND DO.***

Gradually, bit by *'not that noticeable at the time'* bit, all of our lives, our personal details have been handed over to the people who would control and manipulate us. Our medical history, our financial history, our personal history, our absolutely everything! You remember those people who run *the system*? Yes, that lot. The ones who would have us treading the hamster wheel on the road to nowhere...

"Right, all you young trainees, you are ready to go out and con the masses. You have

received all of your training in how to lie, cheat, baffle, confuse. The best of you will remain here with me, while the rest will go forth and spread your wings, fill your pockets, fill your boots. There are positions waiting for you in the property market, in banks, in the legal profession, and in insurance companies. You know how to totally confuse the public with baffling technical jargon, bullshit. Off you go now, and remember the watchword **CONFUSE**! When the peasants are confused, then you pounce! You have the details of every citizen in your database, so go get them!"

"What are the rest of us doing then Sir?"

"The rest of you will become politicians my boy. You have shown us that you have all of the right qualities to become our pets, our favourite little perpetuators of *the system.* We will divide you into nice, neat, little groups and you can debate between you what you think is the best way to perpetuate our wonderfully crookcd, and gorgeously efficient, money making system. We will listen to how you progress, then we will recommend which particular branch of the political wing of the system that you will be placed in."

"But I thought all the political parties had different ideals, different ways of doing things, Sir?"

"They do dear boy, outwardly. Some of them con the masses in one way, while others will do it in a different way. 'Divide and rule' is what we call it. Since the political wing of the system became open to what we like to call more *common* people a few decades ago we had to change our thinking a little, just the odd bit of tinkering, nothing too serious."

"How do you mean, Sir? The Conservatives, Liberals and Labour people in Britain are miles apart from each other. And in America, the Republicans and Democrats are miles apart too!"

"Yes, indeed there are dear boy. This is the way we like it, the way we want it, the way it must be. What use would they, you, be to us if everybody thought the same way? Hmm?"

"Yes, I think I see what you mean Sir."

"To properly execute the divide and rule policy we ABSOLUTELY MUST have the peasants divided, and what better way than to have their so called *leaders* divided?"

"Ah, yes, now I get it Sir. That's very clever, Sir!"

"I know. Right, what we do is this; we allow a certain amount, not too many, of the *common* people into politics. We also allow a few people of, shall we say, *class*, to join in. A few mavericks who want to be *people's champions*, so to speak. Oh yes, there are a few rich people who seem to want to help the peasants along in their dreary lives. We allow these well meaning fools to have pretty much a free run, let them gain a good following, as it were, along with the ghastly *common* people. It helps to keep the peasants in their place you know, keep them believing that someone is genuinely on their side, while they keep that lovely little hamster wheel turning."

"Is that how we keep the balance Sir?"

"It is, dear boy, well done. We keep the balance by making the peasants think that they have people on their side. But they don't, nobody is on their side at all. We allow their so called *champions* to get so far, then they are stuck."

"What happens then Sir?"

"They have to join the higher system or go no further. Some do, some don't. Those that don't, well they just slip back into whatever they were doing before. Those that do, well they become ministers, even Prime Ministers. They then have power, and money, lots of lovely money. But they can only do so much, only say so much. We are the ones that have the real power, the final say. We pay their salaries so we dictate what happens, what they can do, what laws they can impose on the peasants."

"But I thought they were paid out of taxes, the money that we take from the peasants Sir?"

"They are indeed dear boy, but who owns the peasants? Who owns everything that they can or can't do?"

"You do Sir."

"Precisely. We own the peasants, we own the entire crooked system. The system that the peasants are trapped in is ours, every last little tincy wincy bit of it. We own everything, thaty's how we can manipulate everything."

"Right, I get it Sir. The system owns the banks that the peasants are trapped into using and everything that they want to do is governed by whether the banks will give them any of their money back."

"Indeed so dear boy. We own the banks, as you say. We own the legal system, we own the lawyers, the property market, we own the politicians that the peasants think make the rules. We own everything. One of our star pupils is doing very well for himself, and us. He is the perfect example of exactly what I am trying to teach you."

"Sir?"

"Mr. Blair. The peasants call him Billy Liar, he has perfected the art magnificently! There are others, of course. Some are pretty good, others not so good. There are even some that forget their training. They slip into the trap that is laid by some of the less stupid peasants."

"What's that then Sir?"

"They begin to think for themselves. They even start bringing the ghastly F word into things."

"You mean..."

"Don't say it boy! You know the word I mean, and it is banned, forever. If they start doing that we give them titles, peerages, things like that. We move them out of the way. They are all pretty easily bought off. Money and privilege is what they understand best. Right, you know how we control the politicians, the next bit to learn is how we get the politicians to control the peasants. This is remarkably simple, and very easily carried out."

"How Sir?"

"We politicised everything. Absolutely everything! The police force, the education system, the justice system, the health servicfe, it's really quite marvellous. We thought of this several decades ago, but it was very difficult to carry out, initially. Our wonderful Mr. Blair did enormous work in this field, and he did it so well that the fools *in charge* now are carrying on where he left off! It's brilliant!"

"Will it always be so easy though Sir? Will some of those things get de-politicised?"

"No, most unlikely now. You see, all the people who run these things were placed there by us. Mr. Blair achieved the highest mark possible in the number one examination we set."

"What was that Sir?"

"The *BBC* we call it. Bullshit, Brainwash, Con. All of the people running everything are completely politicised, and all of these are, broadly speaking, in the same place politically. They are all slightly left, or just slightly right, of centre. This was our masterplan, and it has worked so fantastically well. We now have everything perfectly politicised, political correctness is right at the top of everyone's agenda, those that run everything, that is. Human rights and health and safety are ingrained in every single law and rule. As we all know, these things are heavily weighed down with stupidity, so it is very easy to perpetuate."

"But how, Sir?"

"Because it ensures that all of our little pets, those lovely politicians, can continue to argue about everything. This in turn leads to all of their daft peasant supporters arguing about everything. It's the *Divide and Rule* that I told you all about earlier."

"Right, now I get it Sir. It's really quite clever, isn't it Sir?"

"No, dear boy, it's brilliant. It's fail-safe. But there is more to it than that. All of the heavily politicised institutions now know everything about, and have unhindered access to, all of the peasants and all of their personal details. They have everyone's health numbers, national insurance numbers, addresses, telephone numbers, email addresses, personal details, clothes sizes, dental records, everything. We know absolutely everything about absolutely everybody and this is how we can so very easily keep them exactly where we want them. Come with me, watch this little film about how we keep watch on the masses."

I think we'll leave them to it, sneaky wotsits. This all sounds worryingly familiar to me, they absolutely DO know everything about us. Cameras are everywhere, it seems. We all log on to the internet, play with social media, as they like to call it. Do we really think it's safe, that it's not a state sponsored way of spying on us? We use bank cards over the telephone, and on the internet. It only takes one little word out of place, and who knows what may happen. Virtually everybody has a mobile telephone now, accept for your ninety three year old Auntie Mary, but they don't care about her because she doesn't get out much these days. It's dead easy for them to track everything you do, everywhere you go, and even what you say. It won't be long before the chip is inserted into our bodies that sends all of our thoughts to the central data base.

"Hello, who's calling please? It didn't show up on my phone as a number, it just said *'call'*."

"That is Mrs. Nobody I presume."

"Look, what do you want? I told you not to call this number again. I don't know what you want or even who you are!"

"You don't need to know, Mrs. Nobody, but to set your mind at rest I will tell you that this is *the system.*"

"What do you want? I don't like this. I'm ending this call now!"

Mr. Nobody is in the next room.

"Who was that darling? On the phone I mean?"

"He said it was the system, they have rung twice now. I don't like it, it sounds sinister. Flick the telly on love, I need to watch something light and cheery to take my mind off it."

Horror! The voice on the telephone is now droning out of the television.

"Oh no! Darling, switch it off I can't bear it!"

"I can't, it won't switch off. The volume won't go down either. Try unplugging it."

She did, but it was still on. The voice was still droning on, they couldn't do anything to silence it. They were unable to move either, transfixed, as if being controlled.

"Mr. and Mrs. Nobody, it is pointless trying to switch me off, or silence me in any way. We are the system, and we have you in our control. We know all of your thoughts, and if you continue to think bad thoughts about us you will be punished."

"What do you mean, bad thoughts? How the hell do you know what I'm thinking?"

"Come on love, let's get out of here. This is scary shit. Someone must have tampered with the television. Let's pop next door and see if theirs is the same."

"Good idea darling. It might be one of the kid's friends from school playing about, one of the computer whizz kids. Hey, the front door won't open, it's jammed! Try the back."

"This won't open either, or the windows! We are locked in, they are keeping us prisoner in our own home! Hey, you on the screen! Whoever you are, get off! Get out of here!"

"Mr. Nobody, you may shout and scream as much as you like, if it makes you happy. You cannot escape. All your actions, your words, all your thoughts are being recorded."

"What? How? You think you are clever, you might know some things about us, but you can't know what we're thinking, that's impossible!"

"There is a microchip in your television set Mr. Nobody, there is one in all your bank cards Mr. Nobody, there is one in every appliance in your home, there is a microchip in the dental fillings in your teeth Mr. Nobody. We record absolutely everything that you do and say. We know your every thought, down to the tiniest detail. We control you Mr. Nobody, we control everybody and everything."

Scary scenario? It may seem a little far fetched at the present, but give them time. You can be absolutely certain that this, or something like it, is absolutely what they do want. You think bad things about the system, you complain, they will alter your thought patterns.

"I – am – an – obedient – servant – of – the – state." Actually, they are very likely preparing the microchip for me as I write this.

"How dare you question our wonderful system and the people that we have running it?"

That's quite enough of that, it scares the living daylights out of me, that scenario, but it may well be closer than any of us fully realise.

Meanwhile, over the channel in Greater Germania, I mean Europe. Little slip there, they haven't *quite* achieved complete control, yet. Over on the European mainland the posturing and word wars are gathering pace. Comrade Field Marshall Bignutski has been put on full alert, to make sure all the troops are ready for when Major Colonel General Largegob Bignuts gets the nod from Mr. President to make sure that all of Europe remains in German, therefore, US control. Have you heard the muppets?

"This is an illegal invasion of a sovreign state. We cannot, and will not, tolerate an illegal occupation of one country by the armies of another country."

"Yes, and we in Britain agree with everything you say Mr. President. We never invade and occupy other countries illegally, do we Mr. President?"

"No Mr. Hague, of course you don't, and nor do we. We will not tolerate Russia invading and annexing Ukraine because if they are allowed to get away with it then they will have their naval bases back and there will be a very real danger that they can challenge American authority in the world. This we will not tolerate. We are the world's policeman, and we need to keep this role in order to be in charge of the world's oil supply."

"Yes of course Mr. President. Whatever you say, whatever you want us to do, we in London will be ready to give you our instant and maximum support."

Hmm... What have the other lot got to say, I wonder.

"Hey, yankee. You can say whatever you like. We have all the gas. You wouldn't dare to threaten us. We will cut off all the gas supplies. Or maybe we will put it in bombs and launch them at you! Anyway, Germany is *our* friend now!"

Loads more word wars going to happen over there yet, that's for sure. Aren't we all just so sick and tired of bitter old men, power mad loonies, sending young men, and women now as well, off to fight other young men and women? All to satisfy the lust for power, the greed that rules in our sick world. Wouldn't it be so lovely if other people, nice people were in charge. People with rather more in the way of common sense in them, rather less in the way of *'we need to prove that we are tougher than you'* in them. I have heard a few murmurs lately, a few rumblings of discontent, I just got the idea something was about to happen, a pretty big thing...

Chapter Five - Fat Chance

"Good morning everybody, and welcome to our brand new government. My name is Marge and I am the new Prime Minister. Allow me to introduce the cabinet. We have Aunty Gladys who is the brand new Minister for Common Sense. She will see to it that political correctness is consigned to the waste bin forever, and Common Sense will be the way forward. Also, Granny Beryl here is now in charge of the country's finance department. Due to centuries of total mismanagement, not to mention the quite incredible amount of corruption that was rife in there, the treasury has been disbanded completely. We have plans to turn it into a rather nice launderette, with a lovely flower garden out the back with plenty of lines on which to hang the washing.

Granny knows all about good housekeeping, having spent a lifetime *watching the pennies*, as it were, so she will be in charge of the nation's piggy bank. Any expense claims will go through her also. Complimentary washing liquid, as well as fabric conditioner, will be provided in the areas previously awash with drunken members of parliament. Yes ladies, the commons bars.

We have disbanded many outdated and corrupt institutions of the former administration, but we will be keeping some of them, in a reformed state. The National Health Service will stay, and will be run by Matron here. Matron was a nurse for many years, and she has seen just about anything and everything that could possibly happen in a hospital. Matron will be replacing all the ridiculous multi-levels of multi-management on top of multi-management. Matron will see to it that *all* tax payers money that comes into the health service is actually spent on caring for patients and keeping hospitals and doctor's surgeries clean and free from infection.

All the banks have been broken up and a new bank has been formed. This will have branches in every single town and village in Britain, and will be known as The Bank. Gambling with people's money has been totally banned, and anyone who tries it on will be jailed. Every company that operates in Britain will have to bank in Britain, no exceptions. Oh, hang on a minute..."

"Help, help, we're trapped, let us out!"

"I am sorry everybody, that muffled noise you can hear is coming from *the other place* as they used to call it. I think they've woken up."

Crikey, what's going on here? Seems like there has been some kind of coup in Westminster. It seems that Aunty Marge and The Women's Institute have siezed control. Well I for one will be more than happy with this, they can only be a sight better than the male dominated corrupt governments we've had for a few hundred years. Those that have sent millions of young men to certain death in *who knows how many* futile wars. Whatever Aunty Marge and co. do, I doubt they will be starting any wars! I wonder what the noise in *the other place* is, the old name they had for The House of Lords. Oh, here's Marge again...

"All members of this place, what they used to call The House of Commons, are securely held in a building quite close to here, they can't get out. All the doors and windows are locked."

"Blimey, how did you manage that Aunty Marge?"

"Easy, we got all the M.P.'s in there by telling them there

were three bombs in here, and one million in used notes in there. Some got trampled in the rush, but the rest got in there. There's no money in there at all, just a skip full of their expense claims and a kettle. They'll be fine, probably arguing amongst themselves as we speak. The other lot next door were having a debate on the health service, but seeing as all bar two of them were snoring loudly, we just quietly locked the door and turned the lights out. They've been quiet for hours!"

We'll leave the occupants of *the other place* for a few minutes, allow them to wake up a bit. I wonder what else Marge and co. have done, what the other plans are. Here she is...

"The politicisation of everything in Britain, that has been a creeping disease for many decades has been completely reversed. The education system, the police force, the legal system, the afore-mentioned health service, everything that politicians had politicised has been freed."

"Hurrah!" A large, collective cheer from all assembled. There's more though...

"Teachers will be allowed to teach, they will be completely free of politically motivated targets. Just do what they love to do and spent many years training to do, teach. The police force have been released from similar shackles imposed by those who would play political games with them. Police officers will return to policing, with common sense. Every town and village will have real police officers patrolling the streets, on foot and on bicycle. Others will be in cars and on motor cycles where necessary, or even in air and river craft, but none will be filling in forms just to comply with politically correct nonsense. Similarly, the same principles will be applied to the health service, the justice system, and everything else that politicians used to score points over each other while playing with tax payers money."

"Hurrah!"

"You will be wondering, possibly, how all this will be paid for? Well it is perfectly simple, really very simple indeed."

"How Aunty Marge? How are you going to provide so many more police officers? And everything else?"

"We will be trebling the amount of nurses and care workers. We will be doubling the amount of police officers. We will be doubling the amount of teachers. There will be many more schools, every town and village will have at least one police station, hospital, doctors and dental surgeries, and every child will be able to attend a school where they live."

"But how are you, or we, going to pay for it Aunty Marge?"

"Easy. We have disbanded the place next door completely, the former house of so called *lords*. We found all the expenses books, and loads of stuff. They were actually paid a fortune just to turn up and sleep!"

Can you believe that? "I'm a little weary, think I'll have a nap." "Oh, okay then, here's three hundred quid!" Anyway, back to Marge...

"With the ridiculous amounts that were paid to all politicians stopped we will have saved the country billions of pounds."

But what will all those poor politicians do now Marge?

"They will all be employed on repairing the roads of the entire country. They have been stealing millions, even billions, of pounds from everybody for decades through fuel duty and road tax. All of it was supposed to go to keeping the roads in a fit state to drive on. We all know they used the vast majority of it for other things, and kept much of it themselves, so now they can do it. They will be supervised by professionals and they will use the proper stuff, not the rubbish they have used up to now, the stuff that last two weeks. It will be done properly, finally, so that it lasts. All of it will be paid for from the monstrous salaries, bonuses and expenses that they will no longer be getting. They will all be paid double the current minimum wage, which is a fraction of what they used to get, so they will not be able to complain. Or if they do, I don't really think too many of us will listen."

I think we'll leave Aunty Marge and the rest of The Women's Institute to thrash out a few more things. We'll pop back and see how they're getting on a bit later. Meanwhile, in that building Marge talked of around the corner, where all the commons mob are locked up. They seem to be, you've guessed it, arguing...

"Well this is all your blooming fault, you damn Tories! All your cutbacks and austerity measures have infuriated everybody. Now look what's happened!"

"No it's your fault, you labour lot created the mess, we are just trying to clear it up!"

"Excuse me, but nobody is trying to clear it up, whatever 'it' is supposed to be!?"

"Ya boo sucks it's all your fault!"

"No it's not, ya boo sucks it's all your fault!"

"Ya boo sucks it's all the liberals fault!"

"Ya boo sucks it's not!"

"Ya boo sucks it is!"

Well ya boo sucks to the lot of them I say. Good thinking by Aunty Marge to get several hidden cameras and microphones in there before the coup, it's all going out live on television and radio. I wonder if everybody watching and listening will feel they have been wronged and let them out... erm...

They can stew a little longer I think, as can the other lot in the other place. It seems Marge and the others have been very thorough, ooh, look, there are live pictures coming through from Buckingham Palace. Crikey, it's Mrs. Queen. Shsssh...

"It is with deep elation in my heart, and I'm certain in the heart of the entire nation, that I am honoured to welcome my new government. I have long admired the sterling work of The Women's Institute and the splendid common sense practices that they apply to everything they do. Excuse me just one moment...   Charles, Philip! If you two don't stop squabbbling I'll bang your heads together! That's better. As I was saying, The Women's Institute have always been a very fine organisation and I am very confident that they will do a marvellous job of running the country in a sensible, fair, common sense way. In these changing times we must all be prepared to change and adapt, to modify our thinking. It is with this in mind that I have asked my government to change another little rule. When I shuffle orf this mortal coil... excuse me, again, I am sorry. CHARLES! Put that back or you will be sent to your room!

Where was I? Oh yes, when I shuffle orf this mortal coil, hopefully not for a few years yet, because my daughter has more sense in her little finger than my three sons put together, you will have a new Queen. Anne will succeed me on the throne of this country. One hopes that this will meet with the approval of my new government. I thank you all, and hope you join with me in wishing them the very best of luck."

Well, her majesty seems to be pretty happy with the new set up, they probably sent her a few pots of jam and chutnies, the odd cake or two as well I should think. Poor old Charlie, mind you he is a bit of a twit. I've always liked Anne, she does enormous amounts for charity and never steps into the limelight to broadcast it. Unlike her brothers, *Airmiles Andy, Dopey Charlie and Even Dopier Edward*. I wonder if the news has spread across the pond yet...

"Aaarrgghh, why did you do it honey? Why did you do this to me?"

"Oh stop whining for pity's sake, the blood has all dried up now. The pain will ease in a few days. They will have to re-name you No-nuts. Ha ha!"

Crikey, seems like the old soldier met his match. Major Colonel General Largegob Bignuts is no more. Well, he has something missing anyway.

This is looking all very exciting now, the news obviously has spread that The W.I. have taken over. Who can blame them? For centuries men have been in charge, for centuries people have died for nothing, in wars started by power mad greedy loonies. Okay, if women were in charge there might be a few emotional moments, a few tantrums, but that's what happens now anyway. They would be unlikely to be going around launching rockets and mortar bombs at everybody, starting wars where thousands, millions of innocent people die. Oh, seems like Marge has agreed to meet a delegation from the place formerly known as *The House of Lords.* We ought to listen to this. It's Lord Scavenger, Tory Peer.

"Ah, former lord scavenger, what can we do for you then? Have you brought a message from your lot? Do you want to negotiate something?"

"Well, no. We've run out of gin next door. We wondered if we could have some on expenses?"

"Yes, well. I think you can just take yourself away Mr. Scavenger. There is no gin here. Best you toddle off home I think, *next door*, as you call it, is going to be turned into a creche for use by the younger ladies in here anyway. Off you go, and if you can wake the others up you can take them with you!"

"Outrageous! This is not democratic!"

"You talk to me about democratic, Mr. Scavenger? Show him out Beryl!"

I think Marge seems to be a natural, and I'd far rather have Aunty Marge running things than what we have had, for centuries. I wonder if this could catch on, if other parts of the world might follow suit...

"You betcha honey!"

Ooh, look! It appears that there's a new leader in America. I guess we should call her Mrs. President.

"That is right. I am the new president. We heard what you

ladies had done over there in sweet little England and we got going ourselves. The Mother's Union and several other organisations over here seized power overnight, well we just gently moved in rather than seized anything."

Crikey, well done. But where are all the senators and congressmen?

"Oh they are all okay, we locked them all away like you did over there with your lot. Hey, we love that idea you have of turning the government buildings into washing places. We'll get on to it right away!"

Well, it seems that the idea has caught on, quite likely the power of the internet and social media. Things can spread in seconds around the planet when an idea catches on. Let's go back and hear some more of Aunty Marge and the new government's plans. Here's Granny Beryl, she's in charge of the piggy bank, so to speak.

"We have much work to do, but here is an outline of the major points of our plan for the financial health of the country, and ALL of those that live in it. As Marge touched on earlier, everything in Britain has been, or will be very soon, de-politicised. The old guard of corruption within the police force has been completely removed, the same with all of the banks and insurance companies. When we looked into it we actually found that so many people have been telling so many porky pies for so long. We actually have enough money in the country to pay for everything that needs to be paid for several times over, and with billions to spare for a rainy day! There is no deficit, not as they have been trying to tell us. There is no need for any so called national debt that needs to be paid back."

Blimey, where was all the money hidden then Granny?

"We found several trillions of pounds stashed away in the vaults of the banks, in cases marked *'public dosh that we nicked. For management and bonuses only'*. We found trillions more locked away in boxes at what they used to call the treasury, marked with *'not for the public, it's ours'* and *'war funds for when the oil runs out and war breaks out over whose fault it was'*. We have long suspected large amounts of skullduggery going on in those corrupt old institutions, and now we know.

We will be completely revamping the armed services. The army will be there purely as a peace-keeping force, to guard our coastline, with The Royal Air Force adopting a similar role. The Royal Navy will also be used for peaceful purposes like transportation of goods to and from other lands, as well as sea and coastal rescue. The vast majority of weapons, bullets, missiles, tanks and other weapons of war will be melted down or just broken apart. With the metal saved we will have super-duper wheelchairs made for disabled people."

Looks like Granny Bcryl has it pretty well worked out. I can hear you saying, though, that this is all a bit far fetched, a bit daft. Well of course it is, there is no way the house of lords would have run out of gin that quick...

We'll leave Beryl and Aunty Marge and the others to thrash out a few more details, but it is a good idea. Centuries of politics and politicians have resulted in hundreds of wars and billions of deaths. And for what? For why? Wars over territories and lands, religion and differing religion, resources that fuel selfish lifestyles, greed, the lust for power. Who started all these wars? Where they started by the ladies of The Women's

Institute, arguing over how much spice to put in a jar of chutney? Er, no. They were started by power mad men. It's only ever been a small minority of men, but always men. Granted, there have been Queens of England and other places, and female presidents and prime ministers, but the real power has always been with men. Bitter men.

If the ladies were in charge there might be a few rules and laws that some men find a bit daft, but it is highly unlikely that those who bear children and make homes would be trying to destroy life. There maybe an abundance of pink, but that must surely be better than an abundance of grey. (Gray, for those across the pond).

Just take a look back through history. The churches and other places of worship were all run by men. Most religious organisations even banned women from the positions of power within them.

"Dearly beloved we are gathered here today to talk of peace and love and how we don't let women become the ones in the pulpit who preach it."

Well, that's finally changed, at last. How long do you reckon before the whole thing changes? Or will power mad greedy men remain in charge all over the world until one of them throws the fire bomb that sets the ball rolling to final, complete, and total oblivion? We'll see. But consider this; every man on the planet has been brought into this world by his mother. Apart from a very small minority of nutters, mothers are generally good and peaceful people. Maybe if this had happened...

"Adolf! You are a very naughty boy, now go to your room and behave yourself. You will not get any dinner and you will not be allowed out until you learn to be nice!"

"Sorry mum."

Yes, well, a fat chance of that, but I'm sure you get the point of what I'm saying here.

Right, that's me done. I sincerely hope reading this little book has provoked some thought, delivered the odd chuckle or three, or maybe even both! All of the opinions expressed in this book are just that, opinions, and not all are even mine. For those of you that had the *sense of humour bypass* operation, never mind, the rest of us had a good laugh anyway. I may return with some more, but for now I must check up on Algernon Corrupticus the Fifth. He and Lord Swagbag were reportedly seen in a little rowing boat headed South, but it was sinking under the weight...

Th-th-th-that's all folks!

Printed in Great Britain
by Amazon.co.uk, Ltd.,
Marston Gate.